balconies courtyards and pots

great ideas for small gardens
by caroline gunter

The Australian Women's Weekly
garden guides

C O N T

Container basics

THE TITLE, *BALCONIES COURTYARDS AND POTS*, IS TO TELL YOU THAT THIS IS A book about plants that are confined in pots, garden boxes, windowboxes, hanging baskets or shallow earth-filled areas that might be based on rock, wood or concrete. Plants grown in designed areas far away from soil, such as balconies and decks, can create a green, bright, restful, private and/or useful space in what was once probably none of the above.

As delightful as our pictures of these gardens are, plants growing in such straitened circumstances need very special attention. The selection of the containers, suitable plants and potting mix are vitally important. Then there are decisions as to the right site for plants, how to set them up to best effect, and the ongoing care required to keep them healthy and looking good. It comes down to common sense, a little inspiration, a lot of watchful care and the enjoyment of your collection. Together these will make the scene of your dreams a reality.

Cummins' garden, NSW, Australia

As much as possible, we've named the plants featured in the gardens in this book, so you can use the pictures for inspiration, as long as your growing conditions are fairly similar. Throughout the book you will find listings of alternative plants that will suit different conditions. Also pictured are techniques to help reduce wind and screen sun. And there are recommended routines to help maintain the scene.

So first, the containers. Pots come in hundreds of shapes, styles, sizes and finishes and are built, moulded, constructed or formed from a large range of materials. As you will see it is the variety, form and arrangement of the pots that creates the scene, whether it's a formal line of perfect replicas or a mix of contrasting pots.

Above: Contained in an old white painted concrete pot stands a variegated cumquat, the recently replenished potting mix mulched with pebbles. Seaside daisy romps around its feet. More bright colour comes from a pot of golden pansies while the variegated liriope repeats the green and cream of the cumquat.
Right: This 'potting shed' collection of useful pots is stored casually against a back fence. Always select pots just a bit bigger than the root ball that is to go into them, as too much potting mix can cause rotting of roots.

pots

The pot should be approximately 15cm deeper and 10cm wider than the rootball of the intended plant. This will allow roots to extend 10cm all round. The top of the root ball needs a light cover of 1 to 2cm of potting mix to maintain air supply to the surface roots. The pot rim should be 2.5cm higher to prevent potting mix and water washing over the rim.

Right: Plants should not stand in saucers of water for any length of time as the effect is the same as blocked drainage holes. Stand them on pot feet or pieces of tile around the pot edge to make sure the water drains away. If a damp environment is necessary stand the pot on pebbles in a water-filled saucer. Here an aloe stands on pot feet for superior drainage. Mondo grass rests on a pebble-filled saucer. Ferns really appreciate this treatment as well.

Left: To guarantee good drainage and healthy plants, line the new pot with pot shards or pebbles before adding the potting mix.

Left: Select pots that suit your environment, be it tropical, classical, cottagey or formal. Make sure they are weighty enough to remain upright in a windy site and light enough to move about if necessary, to change the scene or chase the sun. Large pots will add drama and can stand alone, small pots can be used in lines or clustered in groups. Your budget and design will determine whether you use plastic (cheaper, slower to lose moisture, lighter to move but easily blown over in the wind, and becoming brittle in the sun), metal, wood or the heavier terracotta, cast stone or concrete. Here terracotta is weighty enough to support a palm and tree-like crassula. The red impatiens repeats the colour of the vivid wall plates.

Do not put plants in pots that are too big for them. The container can become waterlogged and cause roots to rot. It's easiest to line the plant up beside new pots and select the one to fit. The pot should complement the plant by harmonising or contrasting with it — in colour, texture or shape. Check that there are sufficient drainage holes in the base so water will not become trapped in the pot and cause rotting of the roots. It is possible to trim out blockages and enlarge drainage holes with a masonry bit on a drill (not percussion action) drilling from the inside in small bites. Make sure the water that does drain from pots will not cause problems such as rotting of wooden decks or floors, staining or slippery slicks on tiles, or seepage to areas below. Saucers under pots will catch excess water but they will need to be emptied regularly to prevent overflow spillage and damp seeping through them to the surface below.

constructed garden boxes

If you plan to build these with wood make sure you use treated pine or a very durable hard timber, and provide sufficient escape routes for water to drain from the box. Nothing kills plants faster than pooling of water in recessed gardens. Line the wooden box with a waterproof membrane like a pool liner and poke plenty of drainage holes in it. If the construction is to be of stone, brick or concrete, provide ample drainage at the base and around the sides to guarantee water will not pool in the enclosure. Apply a 5 to 10cm layer of coarse gravel over the base before adding the potting mix.

windowboxes

These can be any containers that are possible to attach to the windowsill or surrounds, or a wooden box can be specifically constructed for the site. Terracotta or plastic troughs can be purchased and even a collection of single pots or hanging containers can dress a window. Whatever you choose, it should be selected to suit the scene and fulfil the planned use, be it decorative, screening or harvestable. And it must be able to be watered and to drain. Take extra care that it is securely positioned and not likely to flap about or fall in high winds. Remember it can become heavy with moisture from watering or storms. Check regularly that ties are secure and that screws, hooks or bolts are not rusting.

Below: A windowbox will brighten the scene from outside and from within. The heavy terracotta used here has sufficient weight to be steady on the sill and can easily be tended from the pathway. Always check that pots will be secure in wind and rain. Hardy plants like upright zonal geraniums and trailing verbena put on a good show in full sun, but will look ragged and leggy in shady positions. Make sure the growing conditions will suit your plant choice. Annuals, bulbs and dwarf shrubs all are suitable for windowboxes, and green plantings of ivy, box, succulents or mondo grass are also effective.

Left: Dripping water from hanging baskets will be a constant event so do not place them over doorways or areas where moisture will be inconvenient. Hanging baskets need regular feeding to maintain abundant growth. Slow release fertiliser is useful and an additional splash with liquid fertiliser each fortnight should keep things moving. The choice of chemical or organic fertiliser is up to you. Here petunias give a bright summer show. The purple one is the perfumed 'Belle Amour', teaming nicely with the buttery yellow one.

hanging baskets

These absolutely delightful balls of leaf and flower need considerable care to set up and maintain. You are planning to suspend a container of potting mix filled with growing plants well above the protective spread of leaves and soil moisture. Wind can buffet and whip away moisture, new growth, buds and even potting mix so hang them in protected surroundings and water them daily in warm weather and twice a day if conditions are hot. Remember even a cool wind will dry them out. A drip watering system will make things easier as long as it's used regularly, or is computer-controlled to prevent lapses. Hanging containers can be made of wire, coated wire, coconut fibre, coconut and palm baskets, wicker or plastic. Wire forms allow you to plant all around the pot, creating a ball of plants. Plastic dish forms will be more permanent than moss- and teatree-lined baskets and are useful for displaying plants like begonias, fuchsias, succulents or ferns. If the basket needs lining there is a range of materials available, including the traditional teatree bark and sphagnum moss, moulded peat and newer coconut fibre moulded forms. The lining holds the potting mix in place, maintains some moisture and allows excess water to drain away. There are detailed instructions on setting up hanging baskets on page 77.

Above: The generous growth of the grey-leafed *Helichrysum petiolare* intertwines with white busy lizzies and the deep purple/green leaves of cherry pie. Hanging baskets need generous daily watering or a set-and-forget drip watering system to keep them at their best.

Above: This mass of spring colour was planted in late autumn and hung in the cool to chill the soil. The fibre-lined basket had grape hyacinths inserted in slits all around, the bulbs were planted point-outwards. In the top red tulip and double daffodil bulbs were positioned among the hyacinths. As green shoots started to show, the basket was hung in good sunlight and turned regularly to encourage the flowers to grow straight. The effect is enchanting. Behind hangs a generous cascade of a lantana.

Left: A pretty mix of upreaching pink diascia, trailing purple-flowered *Convolvulus mauritanicus* and generous white blooms of busy lizzie are combined with the rich green of curly-leafed parsley. It's a practical and unusual mixture. Pick flowers or wandering stems to keep the shape tidy and when harvesting the parsley, take outside leaves from several plants instead of stripping one bare.

shallow beds

These are frequently placed as edgings or central features on balconies or courtyards and may be recessed at 'ground' level or built up on soil or over paving or underlying rock. Again, it is drainage that is essential.

Make sure there are adequate drainage holes and that the draining water has somewhere to go. Serious damage can be caused to the bed structure or even the building on which it is placed if water is not given an adequate escape route. And waterlogged plants will not survive.

Below: Always check the depth of soil before choosing and placing your plants. There may be deep pockets and there may be very shallow areas that will only support the merest groundcover. Twice yearly applications of fertiliser are recommended to maintain leafy growth, but don't overdo it. The soil in confined spaces can become overladen with the salts of fertilisers, and wilted plants will be your only reward. And you will probably also want the plantings in this position to be semi-permanent and not grow so fast in response to fertiliser that they have to be constantly replaced. Top dressing of the potting soil will be necessary every spring. Add a light dressing of fertiliser at that time. A mulch of bark chips, lucerne or decomposing leaf litter will help keep moisture in. These shallow beds occur in a courtyard, with house footings and underground drainage and services resulting in limited and variable garden space. A built-up bed supports a riot of zonal pelargoniums with massed ranunculus, pansies and lobelia filling in. Extra depth of soil is provided for a standarised fuchsia and a hydrangea by growing them in pots. Potted roses dress the far side.

selecting the right plants

The plants you select will depend on your vision for the space you plan to decorate (to screen, to create a mood, to make a flowery bower, to provide year-round interest, to produce herbs, vegetables or fruit, etc) and will most likely be a combination of several of these. But over-riding your vision must be careful observation and acceptance of the controlling features of the site. Observe the path of the sun throughout the year if possible, or check with your local weather bureau for information about changes of the sun's angle and day length through the year. Observe or make enquiries about prevailing winds and their intensity, and the local temperature range. Climatic conditions become intensified in the confines of an enclosed, exposed or artificial area, as opposed to the normal garden environment. Walls of brick or glass and paved floors also create their own microclimate as heat is absorbed in sunshine, or air is cooled in shade. All these factors, plus how much time and effort you, the gardener, want and are able to spend, must be taken into account.

Right: This flowering show of pots in full sun will provide colour all through the warm months. Bright daisies, geraniums, pansies, lobelias, larkspurs, roses, pinks and begonias are supported by a trailing aluminium plant (flowering pink), grey-leafed snow-in-summer and green fuchsia stems. Keep them all trimmed of dead or withered blooms and leggy growth. Winter in mild climates could feature pansies, primulas, poppies, snapdragons, kalanchoes, aloes and bulbs.

Right: Chosen for a site with only limited sun, this beautiful combination shows how attractive a variety of leaf shapes and colours can be. The large lush leaf is an arum and the grey leaves are the succulent *Kalanchoe pumila*. At their feet are the bright bristlings of a variegated carex with a small-leafed deep green kalanchoe at the base. Both the kalanchoes will start to flower in winter to early spring.

Designer: Michael Cooke, NSW, Australia

plant science

All plants contain a green pigment, chlorophyll. Water is drawn up from the soil by the roots. Light activates the chlorophyll which splits the water molecules, producing oxygen and hydrogen. Meanwhile, leaves absorb carbon dioxide from the air through pores on the lower side of each leaf. The hydrogen and the carbon dioxide combine to produce carbohydrates (sugars and starch), which are then transported through the plant for its growth. The waste products, oxygen and water vapour, are then released by the leaves. Minerals that were drawn up by the roots are involved in the production of the carbohydrate. This whole process is called photosynthesis.

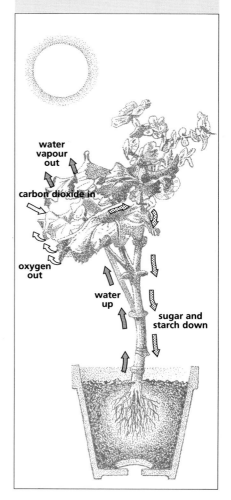

water vapour out

carbon dioxide in

oxygen out

water up

sugar and starch down

Photo: Gil Hanly

A commercial potting mix containing sand, composted organic matter and peat, which combine to provide plant roots with stability, air space and water. Sometimes white lumps of perlite or vermiculite are also included. They are expanded natural materials that will increase the air space or nutrient- and water-holding as needed.

A homemade potting mix with a blend of composted fine bark particles, rice hulls and cocopeat. It's a free-draining soil-free mix that needs good supplies of fertiliser. Well matured compost can also be substituted for commercial potting mixes.

Coarse bark particles make the free-draining mix that orchids and bromeliads require. If water does not drain away from these plants, the roots will rot. Charcoal pieces are often included in the mix.

A fine mix of pebbles, coarse sand and grit create the heavy but free-draining mix for cacti and succulents. Their roots and plant centres rot in wet conditions.

Three varieties of fertilisers: a dry chemical mix, dissolved in water and applied each month during the growing season; polymer-coated fertiliser, slowly released each time the plant is watered; and pelleted poultry manure. (If poultry manure is added to the soil at planting time and covered with a soil topping, it is not so odiferous.)

potting mixes

Any plant that has access only to the soil of its container needs the best soil mix or potting mix available. Don't attempt to skimp here. Garden soil is not sufficient; in the garden it is kept vital with the breakdown of organic material by worms and many other soil organisms, some visible, most invisible to the naked eye. Isolated from this activity the soil loses its structure and becomes block-like. You can, however, use well-matured weed-free compost. This can be very useful for short term displays like bulbs, flowers and vegetables. It will break down too quickly for permanent plantings. Most countries have standardised recommended mixes with approval markings on the package. Buy the best your budget will allow.

Best quality potting mix will combine material to aid aeration, drainage, moisture and nutrient holding, plus have sufficient weight to hold the roots and support the plant. It is available at all nurseries and landscape supply outlets. Don't skimp, either, on the quantity you purchase as there is always a use for any leftover soil, and running out part way through your project can be very annoying.

You can calculate how much mix you will require. For the volume of a box, bed or trough, measure the length, depth and width and multiply these together; e.g. length 50cm x depth 19cm x width 20cm = 19000 = 19L. For a straight-sided round container measure the depth and the radius (half the diameter) and use the formula 3.14 x radius squared x depth: e.g. 3.14 x radius 20cm squared x depth 42.5cm (3.14 x 20 x 20 x 42.5) = 53380 = 53L. For pots with tapering sides, measure the diameter half way down the pot and halve that for the radius, this will allow for the tapering below and the expansion above.

When large quantities are required it is wiser to buy potting mix in bulk from landscape suppliers. If you want to use it indoors, make sure you tell your supplier — some of the outdoor mixes contain composted sewage waste as a wonderful recycled nutrient, but it is not recommended for enclosed spaces.

There are also specific-purpose potting mixes that must be used for plants with other than general requirements. Orchids and many bromeliads, for example, require a fast-draining large-grained mix, usually made of coarse bark particles, perhaps charcoal and occasionally some pebbles. These plants really only need this base for stability in their pots, and as a surface for nutrient retention. Very little moisture is held around the roots of orchids and bromeliads, it must wash past them.

Cacti and succulents also have special requirements. They have their own adaptations to survive in environments with very low rainfall, and success with them in pots must replicate this. Their potting mix is a combination of very coarse sand and small pebbles so water will drain away very quickly.

For plants that require damp soils you can increase the water-holding capacity of standard potting mix by adding extra peat, cocopeat, sphagnum moss or vermiculite.

Left: This zany collection of decorated pots is filled with cacti potting mix and supports an interesting cacti and succulent display. At the back in the large urn is a ponytail, with a stout tree-like *Aloe plicatilus* and grey-leafed panda plant, *Kalanchoe tomentosa* in front. Various cushion and columnar cacti join the group, with a mad purple petunia planted in basic potting mix linking up the colour from the background plants. Finished flower spikes stand tall above the aloe.

Photo: Gil Hanly

planting

When you're transplanting a nursery-bought plant from its existing pot to its new home in another pot, it's important that you do everything you can to prevent transplant shock. Soak the whole pot and the root ball of the plant in a bucket of water. If they are too large for this, let the hose trickle onto the centre of the pot as you prepare the planting area.

1. When planting in a pot, check that the drainage holes are open and that these are sufficient for the size of the pot. Line the base of the pot with crocks of broken terracotta, china, pebbles or charcoal. This prevents the potting mix from spilling through the holes or blocking them up.

In large troughs or planter boxes, cover the base with coarse aggregate or pebbles to a depth of 5cm, then cover this with another 5cm of finer aggregate, pebbles or charcoal.

2. Now the potting mix. Put a 5 to10cm layer of the selected potting mix over the shards, pebbles or charcoal when planting into pots just bigger than the existing pot (see page 6). For a recessed bed or deeper planter, fill with sufficient mix to come to the base of the largest specimen you intend to plant.

Now you're ready to plant.

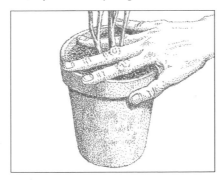

3. Place your hand over the potting mix, with a finger on either side of the plant stem, and invert the pot.

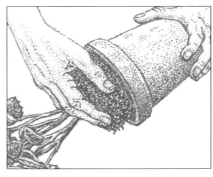

4. Use your other hand to pull off the pot. Do this gently.

5. Tap the rim against an edge, such as a table, if the pot is stuck. For larger plants, loosen around the edge with a knife, lay the pot on its side and gently pull the plant out.

Tapping the pot with a wooden block will loosen the potting mix. Be careful not to tap too hard, especially against a terracotta pot, or you'll end up with shards. To protect your hands from spikes and thorns, when you're transplanting cacti or roses, for example, gently wind a piece of sacking or some rags around the spiky plants before you remove them.

6. Tease out any matted roots.

7. You can use the existing pot as a mould in the new pot and fill around its edges. Lift out the mould pot and place the plant into the space.

8. If the intended pot shape is different, just stand the plant on the new surface of mix and fill around it.

9. To finish the planting fill the pot or container with mix to within 2.5cm of the rim. Tap the pot gently to settle the soil and top up if necessary. Water well to settle the roots in and keep them fairly damp until they are established.

ongoing care

watering

Do not let contained plants dry out to the state of withering — they will probably never recover. Some plants, like coleus, madonna lilies and begonias, will look limp to warn you and recover when watered. But once they go past the limp stage and leaves wither there is not much hope of recovery. Ferns are the startling exception. Their stems are usually at ground level or below, and once the withered, brittle fronds are trimmed off and moisture is returned, new fronds will unfurl again. But there will be none of these problems if you establish a watering regime. It can be a hands-on routine: you and a watering can or a hose going like a bee from plant to plant, pleasantly providing close contact with, and observation of your plants; or you can install an irrigation system.

feeding container plants

Most potting mixes come with a group of fertilisers already added or in an enclosed bag to be freshly combined with the mix at planting time. These formulas will include the major minerals N nitrogen, essential for leaf growth, P phosphorus, for root and stem development, and K potassium, for flower and bud development, plus numerous trace elements that plants need. These will keep plants growing well for a couple of months after planting. Additional fertiliser should be added twice yearly in the proportions recommended on the package, each spring and autumn in mild areas, and spring and late summer in cooler districts. Slow-release fertiliser will provide continual benefits. Always water well after applying fertiliser.

Left: Watering of contained plantings should be regular to prevent plant stress, and deep enough to soak through to the roots. The root ball and all potting mix should be well dampened at each watering. If the water flows out quickly, break up the soil with a stick or digger and slowly introduce water into the holes. Wait for it to be absorbed, enlarging the holes as it goes to the base of the pot.

Photo: Andre Martin

Right: Potted plants that are required to put on a show will need an application of liquid fertiliser each fortnight. Liquid fertiliser is available in organic, (usually seaweed- or fish-based) and inorganic forms (crystals or liquids). All are mixed into water and sprayed or poured onto the plant. As the foliage can absorb the nutrients as well as the roots, it is useful to wet them too. Always follow package directions and don't let the wetted leaves bake in the sun. Apply in the evening.

warning

Over-use of fertilisers can damage plants just as quickly as under-use of them. Too much fertiliser will cause leaves to brown, wilt, blister and wrinkle; growth will be lanky during winter and stunted in summer, and white salts of chemicals will crust the pot and soil. Too little fertiliser will produce weak pale leaves with yellow spotting, slow growth with weak stems, few if any flowers and no resistance to insect or disease attack.

trimming and pruning

These are just normal processes in garden care. Plants outreach their allotted space. They block out the light, close up doorways, lean dangerously and become a problem. Stems, flowers and leaves die and look miserable. All these things occur in a full scale garden and even more ruinously in a contained one. It is best practice to trim plants regularly but gently. There is little need for major surgery, but discreet nips and tucks will keep the scene looking good as well as useable. It will also make the plants live longer and reduce replacement costs.

Leggy outgrowths that spoil the shape of the plant should be pruned back. Conceal the cut among the leafy growth remaining.

Cut off damaged or dead branches to keep the plant looking healthy and attractive, and to encourage it to grow into the right shape.

Above: It's always the frequently used areas of a garden that get the best attention. Particular care is needed with shaped topiary or hedging. These are English box.

repotting

Roots on plants are as important as the stem and leaf section we so admire. But the roots will eventually fill the container. There are two ways to handle this: potting-on and containment pruning.

potting-on

This means moving up to the next size container. It involves the same process as described in Planting (page 14). If roots have gone through the drainage holes you will have problems removing the pot. Snip the roots off if they are small, and prune the stems and leaves to compensate for the loss. In its new, larger pot regrowth will develop rapidly. For large roots you will probably have to break the pot to release them. It is advisable to pot-on in spring, summer and early autumn at the latest, while plants are making vigorous growth. Do not feed for three weeks.

containment pruning

This is used when you can no longer pot-on as pots become too heavy to deal with, too large for the site or the design and too expensive to replace. The process involves pruning of the roots so they can fit back into the container with enough room for new potting mix around them. An equivalent amount of top growth is removed to compensate.

1. Soak the root ball. Get help if the pot is heavy or the plant large — many nurseries offer repotting services. Lay the pot on its side and loosen the root ball with a knife or long piece of flat metal. Proceed as described in Planting (page 14). Once the root ball is removed from the pot, remove the shards that have become entangled in the roots and replace them in the base of the pot.

2. Tease out the roots that have become twisted around and prune them off with sharp, clean secateurs or knife (sharpen and dip them in bleach or use new equipment; damaged or diseased roots can cause major problems). Trim off some of the base and sides of the root ball. A sharp knife is useful for this, carving sections away, reducing the root ball enough to allow 5cm of new potting mix all around.

3. Place potting mix on top of the shards and stand the plant back on it. Check that its top is a few centimetres more than 2.5 cm below the rim and that the base is steady. Fill with additional mix, tap the sides to distribute the mix and eliminate air pockets and spread 2cm of mix over the top surface of the plant. Now there is room for root development in all directions. Water well.

4. Pruning must now be done on the stems and leaves to compensate for the reduced root mass. Always prune back to just above a leaf junction or a new bud as new growth will emerge from this point and sharp stick ends will be obscured. Repeat all round the plant so that its original shape remains but its bulk is reduced. Water it well again and return it to a shaded position to ensure newly exposed leaves do not burn. As soon as it has hardened up, return it to its original site, and re-commence feeding after three weeks. Do not prune roots or stems when growth has stopped over late autumn or winter.

Phillip Bull's garden, NSW, Australia

light

Another of the essentials for plant growth is to provide the amount of light required. All plants need some light but it varies according to where they originally grew. If placed in the wrong position they will either shrivel and blister from overexposure to the sun, or the stems will lean and elongate towards the light source. Place plants in positions where they can grow straight and robust. Refer to the information on the plant when purchasing or use your own or another gardener's experience. Take care when moving or repotting plants that have been growing in shady sites that they are not burnt by inadvertent exposure to sun Most will toughen up if slowly introduced to more light but always bear their original habitat in mind.

Above: Yellow flower and leaf colour always looks bright. The morning-dappled sun here turns to bright afternoon exposure, allowing small French marigolds in yellow and orange to grow with a yellow lantana.

Recipes for success

focus on a single pot

A VERY ATTRACTIVE DISPLAY can be created in a single pot. The drama of a single plant — marking an entrance, used as a central focus, filling a corner or used as an accent on a table — should be scaled to suit its purpose. Large, where impact is demanded and where space will allow, smaller for detailing. Both the pot and its contents are the feature and should enhance each other in shape and colour. Personal taste has much to do with your selection so that the effect will suit your house and your garden. If you are a raw beginner it may be sensible to buy only small examples of

various plants to find out what grows best in your site. Then you can buy the more expensive large specimens to make the impact you require. Having selected the plant, look at all the pots that will most suit the size, colour and shape of your purchase. If unsure, get help from the nursery or landscape staff. Potters often make unusual plant pots and may well provide you with something really special.

A single pot can contain a number of plants to form a miniature garden, with upright growers, trailers and assorted leaf or flower colour combinations. Alternatively, a selection of a single variety can be used, resulting in a mass of leaf or flower colour. The pot must be large enough to contain the mass of roots, and high enough to suit the scale of the arrangement, but will often be obscured by plant growth, so the selection is not quite so critical. The possibilities are endless.

Right: A dramatic Lutyens-styled seat is framed by a pair of daisy standards, simply and effectively contrasting against a clipped box hedge. The daisies in the foreground lead the eye in. Always trim deadheads from daisies to extend their flowering and keep their good looks.
Above: Bronze tones of a strappy-leafed flax and a paddle-leafed ajuga have been paired in a stunning year-bright display.

small bright planting

Here is a jewel-bright collection that will gleam in a sun-soaked or sun-dappled site right through late spring into autumn in subtropical, Mediterranean and temperate zones. The red flowers with purplish leaves are the small bedding begonia, *Begonia semperflorens*. The right colour can be purchased as well-established plants in single pots, usually sold as 'potted colour'. They are also available as smaller plants in punnets, but here there is usually a mixed colour combination and selecting purple-leafed, red flowering plants may be difficult if you want to repeat this pot exactly. They can also be easily propagated at home: merely cut the fleshy stems and plant in potting mix during spring, summer and autumn. Protect through

winter, especially if frost is likely, and plant out in spring. They will grow to 20cm high and round. Trim off leggy extensions (use these for cuttings if desired) to maintain a compact shape, and nip off finished flowers to keep new blooms coming. The little purple and yellow trumpets are wishbone flower, *Torenia fournieri*. These can be purchased as seedlings or grown from seed in spring and planted around the edge of the begonias. Their snapdragon-like flowers start in summer and are followed by interesting purplish capsular seed heads. They tone wonderfully with the begonia leaves. Both enjoy damp soils, so are one of the rare combinations where a saucer of water underneath will not damage the plants. Let the saucer dry out between waterings, then soak the pot and allow it to drain and stay in the saucer. Trim

to tidy and feed with liquid fertiliser throughout the growing season. Remove them from the centre stage before they look exhausted, trim them off, and give them a protected position during winter in mild climates. They can be rejuvenated with new potting mix and a fresh start next spring. In cooler zones they are best treated as annuals, so plant up a new mix in spring.

ASPECT Full or dappled sun

CLIMATE Subtropical, Mediterranean or temperate

WATER A good soak every two days or when water in the saucer has gone

POT SIZE 40cm diameter

PLANTS 4 to 6 begonias, 6 to 8 torenia

pink sun worshippers

Here two pink performers supply abundant trailing prettiness for a pot, planter or basket baking in full sun. This combination will suit Mediterranean, temperate or subtropical climates and flower throughout the warm months. The deeper pink is a trailing perennial, *Verbena* x *hybrida*. They come in many colours so select a pink flowering form to replicate this or ask for *Verbena* 'Sissinghurst' which has slightly richer pink blooms. Plant two in a 40cm pot in spring. The white/pink daisy is seaside daisy, *Erigeron karvinskianus*, another perennial. It spreads ever so gently on lax stems and its daisies will open white and age to pink on the stem ends. You should trim off spent flowers to remove dead seed heads and to encourage new flower development. Plant these as you plant the verbena. For vigorous new growth put in new plants each spring in fresh potting mix. Verbena will grow from cuttings taken in summer and seaside daisy will most probably seed itself about the garden, so you can be self sufficient after the original purchase. Do not over-feed this planting or you will get leaf growth at the expense of flowers. After the initial planting with best quality potting mix, one feed with liquid fertiliser in summer and another in autumn will be sufficient. Watering is also not a major demand: a once weekly soak until water drains away from the base should be sufficient. In hot dry winds you may need to add more.

ASPECT Full sun

CLIMATE Subtropical, Mediterranean or temperate

WATER Once a week good soak

POT SIZE 40cm tub

PLANTS 2 verbena, 2 seaside daisy

a year of interest planting

This small round pot has been placed in full sun on grey decking and will indeed produce an arresting display throughout the year in both Mediterranean and subtropical climates. For temperate zones it will need protection on a sunny deck or behind glass. Standing boldly in the centre is a small plant of dusty miller, *Senecio bicolor*. It looks wonderful on the grey decking but will actually become too large for this planting as it can easily spread to 1m high and round, swamping its partners.

Helichrysum petiolare, also grey, is more amenable, sharing space with other plants and will weave rather than swamp, but will still need control trims. The tuft of green crinkled foliage is a polyanthus, *Primula* 'Pacific Series', which will have displayed heads of multiple flowers in strong jewel colours throughout winter. Some even have a perfume! They will happily flower in shade. If kept relatively damp and well-fed they will probably flower again next winter. Red and white flowers on bronze-

leafed plants are bedding begonias, *Begonia semperflorens* cultivars. In mild climates they will survive through the winter; trim them down as they start to get scraggy and wait for new strong growth to burst forth. If they do not re-emerge after winter in colder climates, replace with new ones. There are pink-flowered bronze-leafed forms if you would prefer that combination. Set to trail over the edges are several lobelia, *Lobelia erinus* cultivars in assorted colours, their purple tones repeating the purple of the cherry pie, *Heliotropium arborescens*, flowering beyond the deck. Buy or grow seedlings of lobelia 'Colour Cascade' or 'String of Pearls' and plant out in early spring. Trim back dead woody undergrowth as they thicken. They will sometimes last longer than a year, otherwise replace in spring. The last neat clump of white is sweet alyssum, *Lobularia maritima*. It will thicken and foam with flowers over the edge all through summer and autumn in temperate zones, throughout the year elsewhere. Trim it back or replace each spring.

ASPECT Full sun or very light shade

CLIMATE Mediterranean, temperate or subtropical

WATER Soak once or twice a week; if under roofing remember it will get no rain

POT Squat shape 40cm diameter

PLANTS 1 dusty miller, 4 polyanthus, 4 begonias, 4 lobelia, 2 sweet alyssum

FEEDING As a semi-permanent planting it will need best quality potting mix to start and a spray of liquid fertiliser every two weeks during spring and summer, tapering off as growth slows. Do not feed during winter but remember to lightly water. Top dress the potting mix with slow-release fertiliser and extra mix to continue the display, or plant out any survivors and begin again with new materials.

spring festival

Starved for colour over the long bleak chill of temperate or continental winters, the first spike of green is a much anticipated delight. The wonderful cheer that colour brings lets every garden designer go a little wild. In this generous dish of spring offerings we have red, yellow and purple, in gorgeous defiance of the rules. This bowl is part of a large park display. It contains tulips, which must have cold conditions with frosts and cold soil to produce flowers. In milder climates it is possible to simulate winter by storing the bulbs for about 8 weeks in the crisper drawer of a refrigerator before planting in late autumn/early winter. For a planting like this with seedlings between the bulbs, leave 10 to 15cm between bulbs with the tops just below the surface of the mix. When you plant a pot of tulips only, the bulbs should be almost touching. There are many varieties of tulip bulbs available. To replicate this pot, select a single red variety to flower in mid to late spring to coincide with the other flowerings. The well-advanced seedlings of red-flowered English daisies, yellow polyanthus and purple viola were raised from seed and grown on under protection during winter. They were added to the pot in early spring once the first leaves revealed the tulip positions. The specific colour selections complete the startling effect of the planting. Deadhead regularly to keep more flowers coming on the annuals and the display will last a bit longer. Feed with liquid fertiliser every two weeks. Remove the bulbs only when the leaves have died down if you want to replant them next year. You could keep this pot going into summer with lobelia or sweet alyssum around the edge and *Salvia splendens* as the tall spikes.

ASPECT Full sun

CLIMATE Temperate

WATERING Keep the soil just moist

POT SIZE 50 to 60cm tub

PLANTS 12 tulip bulbs, 8 yellow polyanthus, 8 purple viola, 6 red English daisies.

FERTILISER Slow-release fertiliser in potting mix, liquid fertiliser every two weeks once seedlings are added

Pictured at Floriade, Canberra, Australia

Tudor garden. Canberra, ACT

volumes of viola

Here is a stunning massed planting of pansies, the small flowering type that were once called violas. This spring collection includes four of the strong-coloured varieties like 'Jolly Joker' or 'Roggli Giants' planted with four of the pinker-toned varieties like 'Wild Silk' or 'Antique Surprise' in the same pot. They all have contrast blotch markings. Check the descriptions on the seed packets or seedling containers to ensure you get a mixed selection. If using seed, plant them in seed trays in late summer in a protected position in full sun, keep them moist and feed them with liquid fertiliser every two weeks after the true

leaves have developed. The seedlings will be ready to plant out in pots in winter, or early spring in cool districts, and will start flowering soon after. The potting mix should be good quality and boosted with slow-release fertiliser. Continue the liquid fertiliser routine once they are planted. Trim off spent flowers and leggy growth to encourage more buds and lateral stem development. Position in full sun for most of the day. This container has been given extra strength by partnering it with a container of *Lobelia* 'Crystal Palace' and another purple cluster in a pot of petunias. The white statue in a bank of grey foliage, lavender or lavender cotton nicely frames the trio.

ASPECT Sun most of the day

CLIMATE Temperate, Mediterranean or subtropical

WATER Keep the roots just damp

POT SIZE 30cm round or square; at least 20cm deep

PLANTS 8 mixed pansies

the richness of red

Red, bronze and cooling green have been combined in a generous tall pot producing a delightful cluster that will gleam all summer long in temperate, Mediterranean or subtropical climates. It will survive over winter and with a rejuvenating top dressing of the potting mix and a hard pruning back of the ivy, salvia and geraniums, it will perform just as spectacularly next year. The stunning strappy leaves are a bronze-leafed cabbage tree palm, *Cordyline australis* 'Purpurea', happiest in slightly moist but well-drained soil. The other bronze leaf belongs to several plants of *Heuchera* 'Palace Purple', a clumping perennial with robust leafy growth and delicate white flower sprays in summer. It will look a bit ragged during winter so trim it back well as leaves collapse. Filling the gaps is a bright red but small-flowered shrubby salvia. Trim back to stem buds about 2.5cm above the pot surface after flowering has finished. A showy geranium, *Pelargonium hortorum*, used here has red double flowers. They will start to flower in spring and, if regularly deadheaded, will repeat well into summer and occasionally autumn. Prune them back well in autumn in mild climates or early spring in cool zones. Cascading over the edge are several plants of a miniature ivy with marbled leaves, *Hedera helix* 'Marmorata'. Regular trimming of the odd longer trailing stems will keep it looking natural and not 'haircut' pruned. The potting mix should have slow-release fertiliser included for the initial planting in late winter or spring. Extra peat or cocopeat will increase the water-holding ability of the mix. Plant the cabbage tree palm in the middle, geraniums and salvia around, then heuchera and ivy at the edge. Water well at least once a week, but more if conditions are very hot. This display is best in full, or at least half a day's sun.

ASPECT Full sun

CLIMATE Subtropical, Mediterranean or temperate

WATER Soak well once a week

POT 35 to 40cm high pot

PLANTS 1 cabbage tree palm, 3 red geraniums, 3 red salvia, 3 *Heuchera* 'Palace Purple', 3 ivy 'Marmorata'

FERTILISER Slow-release in original mix and added again in late summer, liquid fertiliser every month during growing

Photo: Gil Hanly Chenies Manor, UK

Designer: Michael Cooke, NSW, Australia

a contrast of shapes

Wine red pointed leaves of this small-growing flax, *Phormium* 'Bronze Baby', create the central fountain in this arrangement. Clustered around its base are four clipped round 'rocks' of cotton lavender, the grey-leafed form, *Santolina chamaecyparissus*, and green-leafed *S. rosmarinifolia*. A very regular clipping regime will keep the shapes round and leafy. If let grow too leggy between clippings, woody stem-ends become obvious and spoil the effect. Regular clipping also stops the development of the flower heads which must be sacrificed here. This geometric display is planted in a heavy square terracotta pot set amid a display of similar forms, with a rounded echeveria clump in the foreground, repeating the shape and the blue-grey toning. This planting will suit most climates and will happily survive winter, the echeveria being the only one that may need protection from frosts. Turn the pot around regularly in its position in full sun to maintain maximum colouration in the leaves and even growth of the shapes. Slow-release fertiliser applied at planting and each spring and late summer should be sufficient. Water fertiliser in well and give the pot a good soaking once a week.

ASPECT Full sun

CLIMATE Mediterranean, subtropical and temperate

WATER Soak once a week

POT SIZE 35 to 40cm square

PLANTS 1 flax 'Bronze Baby', 2 grey cotton lavender, 2 green cotton lavender

a green and white mound

How to take the stiffness out of the clipped order of box edging? Team it with a centre of uncontrolled gaiety in the form of stars of sandwort, bursting like a giggle in among the sobriety. The box, *Buxus microphylla*, bought at about 10cm high, are planted around the edge of the dish. Trim them lightly as soon as they are planted to encourage the development of new shoots right down the stems. Plant *Arenaria montana* in the centre to produce this spring scene, and a couple of bulbs of white *Colchicum speciosum* for autumn madness. Trim back the sandwort after flowering to keep it in shape and trim the box after each growth spurt. Water regularly and add sphagnum moss, peat or cocopeat to the potting mix to increase its water-holding capacity. Slow-release fertiliser is added at planting time if not originally included in the mix and every spring and early autumn to follow. This collection will respond well to root pruning (see page 16) in its second spring and each one to follow.

ASPECT Semi-shade

CLIMATE Mediterranean, temperate or subtropical

WATER Keep just damp, but well drained

POT SIZE 30 to 35cm pot, height 10 to 15cm

PLANTS 6 to 8 small box, 1 sandwort, 2 white autumn crocus (optional)

intricately moulded

Part of the pleasure of this arrangement is the unusual detailing around the edge of the pot. The other delight is the patterning of the combined plant forms that fill it. There are numerous grey-leafed succulents that mound and multiply. Most are *Echeveria* species. Select to suit. Succulents will thrive in baking sun, dappled shade, howling winds, drought and torrential downpours (as long as the pot is well drained and potting mix free draining), but most will not tolerate frost. Bring the plant in under protection to preserve it (and to preserve this intricate pot too, which could crack in frosty conditions). The delicate strappy contrast is provided by miniature mondo grass, *Ophiopogon japonicus* 'Compactus', planted around the edge. It will be happy in the same climatic conditions but may need an occasional extra watering in very dry spells. It will become necessary to trim back the vigorous development of the succulent to keep the growth from obscuring a pot edge like this;

they can drape over if your pot is plain-rimmed but will still need some controlling trims as they just keep multiplying. Slow-release fertiliser should be watered in well in spring and early autumn.

ASPECT Full sun

CLIMATE Mediterranean, subtropical or temperate

WATER Rain and occasional soaking if mondo grass wilts

POT SIZE As large as you like; smallest 20cm for any effect

PLANTS As many succulents as are needed to partially fill the centre, leave room for spread. Enough dwarf mondo grass to plant at 10cm spacings around the edge

Designer: Peter Stubbs, SA, Australia

celebrating the seasons

You can ring in the seasons with single pots. Prepare them in advance, store them in the wings and bring them out to centre stage when they look their best.

summer

At Christmas, a potted and decorated conifer or a representative of your local Christmas bush could replace your usual entry sentinel. And you can celebrate summer with a large pot of frangipani with yellow-toned sweet alyssum at its feet; a stand of agapanthus, cannas, lilies, or monbretia; a circle twined with stephanotis, or maybe a massed daisy planting, all one type and colour or mixed varieties. For a smaller centrepiece, try massed bedding begonias, petunias, or annual salvias in colours to suit your scheme, or try *Houttuynia cordata* 'Chamaeleon' planted with pink busy lizzie and creeping jenny.

autumn

Autumn can be noted with a pot or trough of autumn crocus or rain lilies; a mass of cyclamen; autumn-flowering snowflakes planted with white nerines or yellow lychoris; early jonquils planted with an autumn colouring grass like *Carex* 'Evergold', *Acorus* 'Ogon' or *Hakonechloa macra* 'Aureola'; a splash of autumnal leaves on a potted japonica, Japanese maple, pear or perhaps on a bonsai specimen.

Above: The opulent flower heads of cannas appear on leafy stems, replacing themselves all summer. Plant several in a large pot.
Left: Rain lily or Autumn crocus, *Zephyranthes candida*, are a spendid substitute in Mediterranean and subtropical gardens for their namesakes of colder climates. Both will salute autumn generously.

winter

Winter can feature a magnolia gnarled and leafless with flower buds about to burst, a witch hazel with its haze of gold blooms, the twisted skeleton of a tortured willow or fig, a glowing wattle, bright grevillea, or an early spot-flowering azalea. Bright jonquils could show in cool zones, with polyanthus, early violas or primulas in milder areas.

Photo: Andre Martin

spring

In spring, there is usually so much in bloom, that a central leafy contrast might be most effective. The solid green of a topiary box, bay or ivy shape looks fresh and lush, and the new greenish-yellow of elm blossom, robinia or gleditsia or the red-toned unfurling of the maple are all welcome in a spring potted garden. However, if your surroundings are only green or grey, a bright mix of spring colours will be essential. Tulips never fail to look stunning if conditions are right.

Above: Heartsease or Johnny-jump-ups, *Viola tricolor,* will present their bright faces in winter in full sun in a mild winter garden, later in cooler climes. They generously seed themselves for next year.
Left: A rich russet combination for spring that will look stunning against both green or grey foliage comes from tulips and violas. Anemone or ranunculus would make a good substitute for the tulips in milder climates.

grouping potted plants

THE ARRANGEMENT YOU MAKE WITH your potted plants will depend on the site, the available space, its aspect and climatic conditions and your style. All these factors influence the success of your display and are worth considering when something doesn't work; it might be too sunny, too shaded, too dry, too prickly or just too boring. Clusters of pots have great potential. They can set the scene, create a feature, obscure unwanted sights, screen sun and wind, provide privacy or produce food. And, of course, they can be purely decorative. Decide if the group is to be symmetrical, with pairs of plants or sets of matching pots. Add some contrasts, in pot or plant shape or in leaf colour and shape, but don't introduce too much variety. Simplicity is an important part of symmetry.

When the arrangement is to become more gardenesque, variety is the key. However, as with any design, repetition of colour, shape or form will link the collection. With a massed planting, different sized and shaped pots will add contrast and provide a way to set plants at a variety of levels. Upturned pots, a plinth or stump can also be used to stand pots on. Wall mounted pots,

hanging baskets and vines will increase the scope of the garden. Check that all the plants are receiving their required amount of light and that one is not screening it from another. Make sure you can reach all your plants to water and feed them, and that they are moveable for repotting, trimming and general maintenance. And in your enthusiastic plantscaping, don't forget that steps, doorways and general space for moving about shouldn't become a fight through the jungle. Formality and impact can be produced with a single pot or carefully paired pots, but grouping allows them to become the garden that might otherwise have been impossible.

Right: This pretty scene demonstrates the delight in mixing pot shape and style as well as leaf and flower variety. A large double marguerite daisy flowers taller than the centrally placed compact brachyscome in a pink form. The clear white regal pelargonium is teamed with chalet daisies and *Convolvulus tricolor,* an annual that provides a splash of blue. The crowning urn contains brightly flowering house leek in early spring, a grey cushion of leafy clumps the rest of the year. Green contrasts come from the acanthus cultivar and a variegated ivy. Such combinations are possible with plants that will suit temperate, subtropical, Mediterranean or tropical gardens — a bright scene in any sunny corner.

Photo: Gil Hanly Rathmoy garden, Hunterville, NZ.

Pictured at Belrose Nursery, NSW, Australia

Above: Symmetrical simplicity is the feature here with four identical pots each filled with the same grass, *Carex morrowi* 'Variegata'. In the contrasting deeply-patterned pot at left is another grass shape, black mondo. The group is linked by the various foliage patterns and the predominance of one. They are clustered around a metal sundial.

Photo: Gil Hanly   Searle and Bettesworth garden, N. Z

Above right: This collection of palms with accents of fiery red begonias looks tropically lush but it was actually pictured in a temperate zone courtyard on the sunny side of the house. The brick paving and heavy terracotta pots provide a snug microclimate. The tuberous begonias, which were protected during winter in their dormant stage, either inside or with a heavy layer of mulch over the pots, will start to shoot in spring as conditions warm, but must have high humidity and sheltered conditions to perform well. New plantings each year will make things easier.

In two neat rows are untrimmed box, a happy combination of formal arrangement and tropical unruly growth. A crassula performs the same duty on the left. Survival of all of this will depend on the watering regime and climatic conditions. A drip irrigation system to each pot is the most reliable and trouble-free way to keep all these plants moist for the warm months of the year, tapering off during cooler times. The damp soil will provide some of the humidity required, but an occasional splashing with a hose may be necessary

in very dry conditions. Palms will need potting-on each year or two with slow-release fertiliser included in the new mix, and liquid fertiliser applied every two months during the warm months. Where palms and red accents are combined in one pot, apply liquid fertiliser every two weeks to the flowering plants, spraying it onto the leaves to keep them growing lushly and flowering well. The leaves will absorb the nutrients but the extra dose will not reach down to the roots of the palms; their growth is too slow to cope with this excess of fertiliser.

Left: Potted salad greens, mizuna, oak leaf lettuce and lambs lettuce look abundantly lush and attractive in their own right but can be harvested a few leaves at a time from the outside edge to make a small salad on its own or to add to a mixed lettuce salad.

Below: Screened by tall attractive shrubs, this table setting is private, protected and delightfully inviting, both to sit in and to view. Lattice provides high screening and is hung with baskets of ivy and a flowering kalanchoe. Tall growth of umbrella trees, conifers, camellias and sacred bamboo produce a varied leafy texture while seasonal accents come from star jasmine, azaleas, gardenias, fuchsia, succulents and a stunning croton.

Kelly garden, NSW, Australia

Designer: Peter Fudge, NSW, Australia

contrasts of shape, colour and size

This attractive arrangement mixes the generous green foliage of *Viburnum odoratissimum*, sculptural fronds of a palm in the background, the small-leafed neatness of a cumquat beside it, and taking centre stage are the orange stems and red leaves of a succulent *Aeonium arboreum* 'Atropurpureum'. The orange is repeated in a small pot of ornamental chillies and a permitted busy lizzie escapee. The secret of a display like this is to cluster contrasting plant and leaf shapes and add accents as the seasons provide them. Call a halt at the right moment, don't keep adding when just so much is enough. With a mixed collection like this, each pot will need its own maintenance regime. The palm will probably be potted-on and eventually root-pruned to control when pot sizes become too much (see page 16). The viburnum is best pruned after its winter flowering to keep it in scale, and potted-on as necessary. The cumquat should be lightly pruned before its spring flowering, but if you

formal feature

This dramatic sculptured arrangement is suitable for a shaded courtyard or protected deck. Only two varieties of plant are used in a geometric design using four pot shapes. The central urn and the two lower round bowls contain white busy lizzie, *Impatiens* hybrids, allowed to stretch and fill the containers. In contrast are the clipped box forms: Japanese box, *Buxus microphylla*, lighter green in the biggest pots, and English box, *Buxus sempervirons*, with its more pointed leaves newly clipped and forming two rounded balls in the front (see page 62 for information about shaping and maintaining topiary). The busy lizzies need a splash with liquid fertiliser every two weeks during spring and summer, with one last application in autumn before growth ceases during winter. Trim leggy growth when they have stretched too far, nipping back to a side shoot on intermittent stems. They should not appear trimmed like the box. Box grows best with applications of slow-release fertiliser in spring and late summer. Remember to keep up the trimming after each growth spurt, so you won't have to cut into woody stems. The front pots are draped in babies' tears, *Soleirolia soleirolii*. This planting enjoys a semi-shaded position and a fairly moist potting mix.

ASPECT Semi-shade

CLIMATE Mediterranean, temperate or subtropical

WATER Keep soil moist. Note these pots do not have pot feet to aid drainage. They enjoy the held water.

POT SIZE A generous urn and plinth to hold it, 2 large pots for large box, 2 round tubs approximately the width of the smaller boxes, and 2 contrasting slightly smaller bowls for busy lizzies.

PLANTS 2 English box, 2 Japanese box, 7 white busy lizzies, 3 for urn, 2 each for front bowls

Brian Donges' Garden, NSW, Australia

miss this it's possible to prune back lengthy stems but still maintain the fruit. Pot-on or rejuvenate the mix as required. These will all need regular feeds with slow-release fertiliser and would benefit from occasional splashings of liquid fertiliser through the growing season. The succulent needs fertiliser only twice a year in spring and late summer. The chilli is given general fertiliser to bring it up to flowering and fruiting and then rested for another season.

ASPECT Semi-shade

CLIMATE Subtropical, Mediterranean or temperate (remove the succulent to prevent frost damage)

WATER Soak once per week

POT SIZE Varied

PLANTS *Viburnum odoratissimum,* cumquat, *Aeonium arboreum* 'Atropurpureum', ornamental chilli

Seddon garden, WA, Australia

a dramatic pair

These two delightful Ali Baba jars or pithoi show off their shape with small plantings of succulents in their mouths. Placed on generous steps beneath a garden wall, they dramatically dress the entrance to a sunbaked courtyard. The important part of this setting is the contrasts of colour, shape and growth habit of the plants. The foreground plant with its grey pointy leaves has a sprawling shape. The plant behind has rounded green foliage and upright growth. There are many succulents in this book that will suit such a planting, and many more are available in nurseries and cactus and succulent suppliers. A few words of warning. First, succulents do not usually tolerate frost, so will need the protection of eaves or shelter if this is likely, but generally this planting will suit Mediterranean, temperate and subtropical zones. Secondly make sure the pots have drainage holes, a must for succulents. Fill the bottom half of the pot with gravel or pebbles before topping up with potting mix, and the drainage will be excellent. The third warning regards the

shape of the pots and the roots that grow in them. To remove a well-established plant, soak the soil very well before gently twisting and teasing out the root ball. Succulents don't develop very thick root systems and should be removable. However, the roots of shrubs will fill the pot and you'll need to break it for their removal. If the pot has a mouth wide enough it will be less troublesome to stand the original container either on gravel, potting mix or even just resting in the mouth. The little softening groundcover is *Cymbalaria muralis* which really likes a bit of shade and a cool root run. In hot, baking conditions try snow-in-summer, seaside daisy or a matting sedum.

ASPECT Full sun or part shade

CLIMATE Mediterranean, subtropical or temperate

WATER Minimum

POT SIZE Large enough to make an impact on the site

PLANTS Succulents of differing shape, colour and form

Designer: Peter Fudge, NSW, Australia

sunlight-splashed

A large pot at the back holds a purple-flowering clematis which clambers over a screen reaching for the sun. The tall spires of pinky-mauve clary sage, *Salvia sclarea*, stand above their broad velvety leaves in a pot behind. The smaller purplish flowers with neat grey foliage on the left are a rock rose, *Cistus*, which will keep flowering through summer and autumn. At the rock roses' feet is a variegated hebe, *Hebe* x *andersonii* 'Variegata', with delightful cream-edged foliage and lilac blooms through summer and autumn. A smaller-leafed miniature white flowered *Hebe buxifolia* is in front. The large purplish strappy plant at the centre is *Cordyline australis* 'Atropurpurea'. Twining through its base is a nasturtium, *Tropaeolum majus* which, unlike its yellow-flowered neighbour in front, has deep-coloured leaves. More soft grey is provided by a pot of *Plectranthus argentatus*. The central

Murray garden, B.C., Canada

low-maintenance formality

There's only a wall, paving and a set of pots, but their arrangement is structured and formal to suit the style of the house. Three cast stone half-wall pots have been lined up symmetrically between two doorways. The wall is dressed with an evergreen tracery of delightfully exuberant creeping fig, *Ficus pumila*, with its climbing adhering stems dressed in heart-shaped juvenile leaves. It must be trimmed regularly to stop it from wandering where it's not invited or breaking out into its adult thick-stemmed and thick-leafed form. Nip out new growing points as it's getting established to promote a wide fanning spread like this. The suckering feet will leave a mark on the wall when they are pulled off, however a rub with coarse sandpaper will remove them and if necessary the patch can be repainted. Creeping fig is frost-tender. Star jasmine could look as formal if given a framework to twine around, alternatively espaliered fruit or camellia could substitute in cool climates. All will need regular trimming. Draping lightly over the edge

is mondo grass, *Ophiopogon japonicus*, providing a contrast and softening to the arrangement. To plant, fill the bottom third of the pots with gravel, pebbles or crocks for drainage, and top up with best quality potting mix. Plant one creeping fig at the back of each pot and three mondo grass plants around the front. Feed with slow-release fertiliser at planting if it wasn't already in the mix, and each spring and early autumn to follow. Remember that pots under eaves very rarely get rain, so water them regularly even in wet weather. A good soaking once a week should be sufficient. The central plaque makes an interesting break in the patterning of the wall. Both plaques and pots are available through good nurseries or pot supply shops.

ASPECT Full or dappled sun

CLIMATE Mediterranean or subtropical

WATER Soak well once a week

POT SIZE 30 to 40cm high half barrels

PLANTS 3 creeping figs, 9 mondo grass

mixed pot contains a russet-leafed geranium, *Pelargonium* 'Vancouver Centennial', another basic red-flowered geranium, trailing ivy and *Verbena tenera*. Grey- and red-leafed succulents keep the colour moving at the back

ASPECT Full sun

CLIMATE Temperate, Mediterranean or subtropical

WATER Clematis will need frequent watering; once weekly for the others

POT SIZE Assorted

PLANTS Purple-flowering clematis, clary sage, rock rose, variegated hebe, white-flowered hebe, red-leafed cordyline, assorted nasturtiums, silver-leafed plectranthus, *Pelargonium* 'Vancouver Centennial', red-flowered geranium, *Verbena tenera*, ivy

Henderson garden, Canberra, Australia

a posy of pansies

This small grouping is another exercise in arrangement, just one plant variety in an assortment of different sized and patterned pots. They are all terracotta, richly orange to contrast with the purple tones of the pansies. The artful trick is to display them with two empty large jars, thus circling the pansies with orange. These small pansies, formerly named viola, are a mix of splotched-face types in traditional and pinkish tones. Plant as seedlings in rich potting mix in autumn and allow to develop during winter in full sun. Liquid fertiliser every four weeks will boost their development. In mild climates they will start flowering in winter and in spring in cooler zones. They can survive over more than a year but do tend to get very straggly. In a feature position such as this it would be wise to

replace them with summer-flowering annuals, perhaps globe amaranth, salvia or petunia, maintaining the purple scheme. For a cooler look try white-flowering petunia, short-growing nicotianas or Californian poppy. In this scene the background is screened with conifers and the large leaves of a bull bay magnolia provide cool contrast to the paving. The tiny blue stars in pots and troughs are *Ipheion*, a winter/spring small bulb.

ASPECT Full sun

CLIMATE Mediterranean, temperate or subtropical

WATER Keep from drying out

POT SIZE Assorted

PLANTS Assorted pansies/viola, mixing purple and pink tones

Designer: Harris Hobbs Landscapes Canberra, Australia

symmetrical simplicity

'The same' are the governing words in this arrangement, a line of the same pots, spaced at the same distance, each filled with the same cluster of plants. Gleaming brightly are white cosmos, usually marketed as 'Purity'. They have been encouraged to branch out thickly by nipping out the central buds as the plants grow. Tiny pink compact daisies are *Linum grandiflorum* 'Bright Eyes' which started to flower earlier in spring. Strong purple accents come from early-flowering *Verbena tenera*, which will drape itself among this planting throughout summer. The tall, now leafy growth is *Nicotiana*, just coming up to central buds. The trumpet-shaped flowers are sweetly perfumed. Put all these plants in as seedlings in early spring, positioned in full sun and protected from late frosts. Let them settle for four weeks into the new potting mix with its own slow-release fertiliser, but from there on feed them every two weeks with liquid complete plant food. Turn the pots regularly so a new side faces the sun. Water every couple of days, allowing the mix to just become dry before soaking it again. The verbenas can be repotted for next year or planted out after the display is over. The other plants are annuals and will not last over winter.

ASPECT Full sun

CLIMATE Mediterranean, subtropical or temperate

WATER A soaking every 2 or 3 days, allowing soil to just dry out between waterings

POT SIZE A set of heavy terracotta or cast stone matching pots at least 30cm in diameter

PLANTS PER POT 1 nicotiana, 2 white cosmos, 2 *Linum grandiflorum* 'Bright Eyes', 2 verbena for each pot

pretty maids all in a row

Above: Newly planted out red ivy-leafed pelargoniums give promise of cascading from their pots to join the Virginia creeper on the wall. The neat symmetry of pot and plant shape creates a pleasing wall topping and balances the fluidity of iris leaves in the pool below. There is a touch of humour in their pairing with the languid mermaid fountain and her wry smile. The water

surface grows a pretty cover of small bright green duckweed. Remove enough of this cover regularly to make sky and mermaid reflections possible.

ASPECT At least half a day's sun
CLIMATE Mediterranean, temperate or subtropical
POT SIZE Set of symmetrical squat pots 30cm wide
PLANTS 1 pelargonium per pot

Robin's Nest, Brentford, Canada

suggested plant groupings

in sun

For grey-leafed and blue flower contrast: *Helichrysum petiolare*, *Crassula falcata* or *Crassula arborescens* and *Plectranthus argentatus* teamed with tiny ipheion growing through blue brachyscome, strappy agapanthus and wandering blue plumbago.

Lime green and white: *Helichrysum petiolare* 'Limelight', 'Green Ice' miniature rose, white daisy, yellow flowering shrimp bush, yellow-leaf geranium, crinkly leaf *Viburnum odoratissimum* with hoop petticoat daffodils and white alyssum.

Pink tonings: *Trachelospermum* 'Tricolor', 'The Fairy' miniature rose, pink primula in winter replaced with pink petunia in summer, seaside daisy.

Green, grey and white: *Grevillea* 'Moonlight', *Pelargonium tomentosum*, *Pelargonium crispum* 'Variegatum', clustered agaves, a white-flowered geranium like 'Wedding Day' and *Zepheranthes candida*.

White with contrasts: *Magnolia stellata*, *Abelia x grandiflora*, white lilies both summer flowering and belladonnas for autumn, white nicotiana for summer, white pansies for winter/spring.

Purple-red toners: purple-leafed cannas, chocolate vine or cup-and-saucer vine twining up a support, red-flowering and purplish-leafed *Hibiscus* 'Andersonii', *Vitex trifolia* 'Purpurea', purple-leafed alternanthera, red-leafed dwarf dahlias.

Grey combination: silver pear, cherry laurel, dusty miller, *Convolvulus cneorum*, *Helichrysum petiolare,* grey-leafed nutmeg-scented geranium with white and green iceberg rose, agapanthus and spring violas. To add pink tones, use autumn crocus, mallow or petunia. For yellow, use daylilies, gazania, daffodils or Californian poppies.

in semi-shade

Yellow-green tones: bay tree, golden-leafed mock orange, green goddess arum, *Ligularia tussilaginea* 'Aureo-maculata', white busy lizzies.

Pink with contrasts: pink-flowered cane begonia, twining *Mandevilla* 'Alice du Pont' and hoya, *Begonia fuchsioides*, purple-striped maranta and purple-pink variegated coleus.

Cooling greens: treefern, fruit salad plant, white-flowered cane begonia, variegated ctenanthe, Indian ginger, assorted ferns.

Pretty tones for cooler areas: pink-flowered camellia, Japanese maple, mop head and lacecap hydrangeas, mixed coloured lobelia, white-flowered fuchsia, twining clematis, variegated daphne and white dicentra.

Above: Pictured above is a lime-green and white combination, which will be happy in a sunny position and will give you a year-round display with a group of pots. A freesia was added in lieu of a hoop petticoat daffodil.

in deep shade

Green is the major colour in deep shade but variation is available if you mix different leaf sizes, leaf surfaces and heights of plants. Splashes of colour can be added by introducing flowering plants from semi-shaded areas and swapping them as the flowers reduce.

In tropical, subtropical and Mediterranean climates use the drooping shiny leaves of weeping fig to contrast with any of the cordylines, variegated dwarf schefflera or fatsia. Try palms like parlour palm, rhapis and *Reinhardtia gracilis*, with monsterio clambering about, and ferns, aspidistra, marantas, calatheas and bromeliads at the base. Trailing native violet, babies' tears or *Lobelia trigonocaulis* can provide groundcover.

In cooler zones use treeferns to droop, broad-leaf cabbage tree for strappy shapes, mahonia and cherry laurel for leafy bulk. Parlour palms and rhapis will survive if given protection from frost and snow. Gold highlights can come from gold dust plant or *Fatsia japonica* 'Variegata' with a yellow grass, *Milium effusum* 'Aureum'. Many ferns survive cool shade and pulmonaria and tiny-leafed *Arenaria balearica* could provide low groundcover.

On the left is a purple/pink combination for a shady site. Pictured are maranta, several begonias, a fern, coleus and the purple leaf of a bromeliad.

Planting for all seasons

PLANTSCAPING A DECK OR BALCONY TO EMPHASISE RATHER than struggle against the seasons will pace you through your year, helping you observe the weather, delight in its variety, appreciate its proclivities and vagaries and anticipate its changes. There is a lot more work involved with something like this than with a static green scene, but the results are a lot more exciting. Don't make an impossible task for yourself by aiming for plants that do not usually grow in your climate. Design your plant arrangement to suit your use of the area, with space for outdoor living in the warm months, and a sunny sheltered spot in winter.

Above: Bright summer madness in yellow and red tones results from plantings of Alaska and red-flowered nasturtium seeds which were sown once frosts ceased, teamed with rust coloured *Gaillardia* 'Goblin' and yellow *Rudbeckia* 'Becky'. More clear colour gleams from the yellow tecoma flowers and red pelargoniums with clipped box as backdrop.
Right: The terrace has been consistently dressed on both sides to create more impact from the plantings. From this angle a topiaried bay stands sentinel by the windows and a pair of *Banksia spinulosa* 'Birthday Candles' burn structurally on either side.

Douglas garden, NSW, Australia

spring

Spring sees the leafing up of the climbing hydrangea, *Hydrangea petiolaris*, as it scrambles up the wall it has been secured to. You could also try *Schryzophragma hydrangeoides*. Both do best in cool zones, but Virginia creepers, *Parthenocissus tricuspidata* or *P. quinquefolia* and ornamental grape, *Vitis vinifera* 'Purpurea', or wisteria, will all stand in for subtropical and Mediterranean zones. They will all need regular pruning to control their spread. In tropical zones try hoya, stephanotis or white flowered mandevilla. The tortured willow bursts with lime yellow anthers on its catkins that were a feature through the last of winter. Hazels, elms and maples also carry interesting catkins. A standard wisteria grows in a pot of *Anemone blanda*. Sweet alyssum, violas or primulas could substitute. The straight single stem ensures light and air can move freely about and the topknot can be arranged to obscure unsightly aspects. See page 60 for instructions on topiary trimming. On the table providing another dash of yellow are hoop petticoat daffodils, *Narcissus bulbocodium,* in matching pots that were planted up in early autumn. They can remain in the pot until they become crowded (then divided) in cool zones but in milder areas will need chilling in the refrigerator for at least six weeks each year to simulate winter. Always leave bulbs until their leaves have died down as it's the leaves that will nourish the bulb for successive flowering. A bunch of Queen Anne's lace adds decorative fill when moved from inside. On the paving are small pots of white-flowering bulbs including clusters of star of Bethlehem and taller *Allium neapolitanum* which stand about 30cm high. *Allium karataviense* is a contrasting broad-leafed variety to try. Growing smaller than any of these are white grape hyacinth, or as an alternative, crocus. In warmer zones try white or blue ipheion, snow flakes or chincherinchee. A neat round of spurge provides more lime/yellow contrasts alongside the grey-leafed lavender cotton. Both of these do well in most climate zones. On a stand a pot of meadow saxafrage, *Saxafraga granulata* gives more soft white flowers and the wall has pots of forget-me-not, viola and bacopa. White flowering violas, chalet daisies or busy lizzies could look just as effective in any of the pots.

summer

Summer's new colourings of mauve and purple have highlights of red and bring more density of leaf growth. Along the deck edge is an orderly row of alternated purple- and green-leafed oxalis with a trough of *Petunia* 'Million Bells' which will be decked in purple through summer and into autumn. Browallia or torenia could substitute in warmer zones. A tub of white-flowered potato vine has been trained into a cone and makes a delightful and long lasting green and white mass. At its feet is a dwarf white dahlia. Touches of red appear on the cane-stemmed begonia, which was protected from the winter chill, and the wall pots replanted with busy lizzies. A repeat of the purple leaf colour comes from a smoke bush, filling out the space near a fruiting fig. On the table stands grey contrast of *Sedum bellum* and blue-flowering Russian sage. The fine-leafed willow has been moved against the wall. A generous pot of duranta flowers strongly in the front corner. Take the time to trim off the yellow berries that form in autumn if children use the deck as the berries are poisonous. Substitute with an abelia, cistus, grevillea, salvia or rose perhaps for a safer display. All will need a controlling prune if they are to brave the winter. During hot summer days all of these potted plants will need extra care with watering and mulching to keep them healthy and flowering generously. Stressed plants not only look pathetic but are more prone to insect and disease attack. Check the moisture content of the potting mix by poking your finger right into it. It should feel damp for the plant to survive a hot day. Soak the plants well at night or in the morning if fungal diseases are likely to be a problem. Shade from an awning or umbrella will be necessary for the users of the deck in summer. However, when the deck is not peopled, allow the sun to keep foliage and flowers coloured and blooming.

Photo: © Libelle

autumn

Autumn tones include russet and creamy yellow with the fading green and purple leaf
colour. A variegated physocarpus reaches out
in the corner where the potato vine stood. A
row of russet coloured violas fills the metal
trough, with a container above of autumn crocus flowering as they lie in leaf litter. They will
be planted into pots after the flowers fade to
nourish the bulbs for next year. Alongside on
the shelf is a small pot of *Abelia* x *grandiflora*
with glossy leaves, small white bells and tan
calyxes. As autumn progresses odd leaves
become red or purpled. It will grow into a
good-sized shrub, attractive all year.The blaze
of colour below is a dwarf nandina, an evergreen which remains compact and colours
from its usual limey-green to these red tones in
autumn. Alongside is star jasmine, its glossy
deep green leaves tinting purple in the cool. Its
warm-season white flowers are sweetly scented and it could stand in for the potato vine for
two seasons. Deep green contrast comes from
a large leafed photinia with *Cornus florida*
'Daybreak' providing taller variegated foliage
with autumn colour. A sasanqua camellia, the
willow with golden foliage or the smoke bush
with red tints could have stood in. On the wall
the fading heads and yellowing leaves of the
climbing hydrangea look dramatic with a vase
of autumn leaves and berries as centrepiece on
the table. A platter of chestnuts provides more
seasonal interest. Ornamental grape and
Virginia creeper as substitutes on the wall
would be well coloured and would tone with
the golden violas that fill the wall pots. At the
balcony edge upright leaves and purplish grass
heads of *Pennisetum alopecuroides* contrast
with purpled leaves of a deciduous azalea,
Japanese maple and the Judas tree, *Cercis
canadiensis* 'Forest Pansy'. The standard wisteria would also be golden-leafed and could be
underplanted with white flowering violas or
rain lilies in milder climates. Established jonquils
flower now in mild areas and Eucharist lilies in
tropical zones. Red and cream variegated
foliage of *Houttuyania* 'Chameleon' provides a
repeat of the tones before it dies down for
winter. It must have very wet soil and is happy
standing in a water-filled saucer. Leaves that
fall are collected and composted in pots for
summer mulch. Watering can be reduced as
plants are no longer growing vigorously but
take care if drying winds accompany autumn.

Photo: © Libelle

winter

The starkness of winter allows the tracery of
bare branches and vines to pattern the white
walls and sky. Framed by green and a large-
leafed variegated ivy the scene is cool toned
but richly patterned. The ivies will be heavily
control-pruned in spring as the other vines
become leafy. The slender trunk of the willow
drapes its furry catkins about while snowdrops
and mauve crocus decorate the stand. In
milder zones snow flakes and primulas flower
well in pots through winter. In the corner a tub
of *Viburnum tinus* glows richly pink with furled
buds that will open to flat heads of small white
blossom. On the table is the winter bleached
pot of pennisetum, more snow drops, crocus
and two varieties of hellebores. Limey/white
blooms are *Helleborus orientalis* with its leaves
removed before the flowers open producing
this flower prominent effect. As the flowers
fade new leaves develop. The limey-green
flowers with dark seaweed-like foliage are
Helleborus argutifolius. On the floor is a winter
weathered pampas grass. Pink blossoms start
to unfurl on the deciduous *Viburnum bodnan-
tens* 'Dawn' and pink leafy *Helleborus orientalis* adds another touch of pink. Substitute scented flowering apricot, *Prunus mume*, or cherry
plum, *Prunus ceracifera* 'Nigra' which will provide purple leaves through the warm months.
Daphne and camellias will also suit. In milder
zones cream coloured poinsettia, azaleas, gre-
villeas and wattle will flower. On the table a
metal dish holds food for winter birds.

summer

In this Mediterranean or subtropical balcony the climate changes are more simply but still excitingly stated. Lushly flowering pots of petunias hold the stage on the central plinth in summer, flowering white and purple in bright contrast to the tiles. The bright yellow rudbeckia provides another brilliant contrast under the fruiting grape.

Above: Petunias need regular trimming to prevent the stems becoming too leggy.
Right: The tree-like crassula in an attractively shaped pot has busy lizzies at its feet.

winter

Photo: Gil Hanly Van de Puten courtyard, New Zealand.

During winter the pruned vine leads the eye to the spires of conifers while the bonsai-like crassulas flower. Agaves provide more shape and leaf contrast. The petunias have been replaced by primulas, predominantly white, with an additional pot of carmine and another with carmine centres. The winter yellow splash will come from the calendulas about to bloom.

Above: *Agave attenuata* has silvery grey foliage and a stunning rosette shape.
Right: Fan aloes also have interesting form. In spring they produce tall flower spikes.

Something special

water feature

In the enclosed space of a courtyard or balcony, the sight or sound of water can be a delight. The smooth surface of a pond becomes a mirror reflecting the sky: bright sunlit blue, moving with clouds or streaked with the colours of sunrise and sunset. At night there will be stars and the path of the moon. Alternatively, you can arrange your house or garden lighting to shine onto the surface of the pond, creating a focus to be viewed from inside the house, or from the deck or courtyard. The effect of rain as it tentatively dimples the surface of your pool at first, becoming craters, splashes and overflowing waterfalls in a downpour, can be an exciting contrast to the former mirrored surface, so if possible, make your water feature observable from a window or sheltered spot. The container is important if it is to be seen, but it can be simple. A half barrel or a small dish (a glazed bowl or a terracotta saucer) can be sited to reflect leaves, float flowers and become a pool of light in any quiet corner. A larger receptacle will, of course, be heavier, and will need some consideration in its placement.

Right: This tiny pool is set in sandstone flagging in a courtyard, producing a square sheet on which leaves and petals float and the movement of the sun and clouds are reflected. It is only 30cm deep but its dark lining makes it appear deeper. The decomposing leaf and flower debris at the base are scooped out and used as a mulch around plants. Note also how the paving slopes slightly away from the edge of the pool so excess water can flow into the garden. Repeating the square of the pool is a skirt of mondo grass, *Ophiopogon japonicus*, backed by a well-filled hedge of box, *Buxus sempervirons*. Native violet, *Viola hederacea*, rambles among the mondo. Lush looking white arum lily, *Zantedeschia aethiopica* , keeps its strong green leaves all year if kept damp and conditions aren't too cold, with the dramatic flowers unfurling in spring. A row of white camellias and a large pink one on the right provide winter/spring colour, repeated in a froth of similarly-coloured busy lizzies, *Impatiens* cultivars, just ready for a neatening trim. All these plants are best in semi-shade and will suit temperate, subtropical and Mediterranean courtyards, as long as soil can be kept damp.

Designer: Peter Fudge, NSW, Australia

Left: A bowl has been placed on a bed in a courtyard under the shade of a flowering pear tree. Bronze-leafed *Anthricus sylvestris* 'Ravenswing' and *Ajuga* 'Forest Giant' lean over it at the back with the strappy leaves of a daylily and shapely geranium foliage softening the front.

Below: Calm, serene and wonderfully solid, a stone trough like this is very heavy, but safely placed here on bluestone paving. The black painted lining is a nice foil for the floating flowers, but the deep coolness is revealed with white gravel on the base. Fountain grass, *Pennesetum alopecuroides* softens the edge, supported by bundling yarrow and thyme. An espaliered apple dresses the fence.

Contained water is delightful but it can be the cause of floods, slow leaks, rotting wood and structural damage. All of these can be expensive and hazardous. If placing something on a wooden deck, check that the structure underneath can carry the load. This is only part of the problem. Next is the destructive power of continually damp conditions. Water will always spill and overflow and even glazed pots can seep or hold water around their bases. Treat the wood underneath generously with bitumen or paint to waterproof it and place the container on pot feet or a wheeled base to provide air between the two surfaces. However. these precautions are no guarantee. It is advisable to move the container to a new position regularly and check the condition of the materials underneath. On roof gardens, extra care is essential, both on account of weight and of seepage. Don't attempt a roof garden until you're certain your conditions are suitable.

Designer: Maze Gardens, Vic, Australia

54

Left: A bowl shape dug out of the soil has been sand-based to smooth out the surface and prevent damage to the liner which goes on top. Various-sized pieces of garden rock secure and obscure the edge of the liner and produce a natural effect. They also provide frogs with an entry and exit stage should you be lucky enough for them to find you. Their tadpoles will dine on any mosquito larvae. Over the surface of the water is the ever expanding water fern, azolla. Remove some every so often so the sky will reflect but leave sufficient cover for the tadpoles. Surrounding plants include native violet, a drooping sedge, colourful coleus, feathery artemesia and strappy mat-rush.

Seanna McCune's garden, NSW, Australia

Designer: Faulkner and Chapman, Vic, Australia

Above: A distinctly dramatic Moorish-styled courtyard plays its main hand in water treatments: splashing streams, waterfall and a long tank of reflective stillness. Minimalist planting provides just enough contrast and shadow. A pair of fan palms, one flowering, are underplanted with mondo grass, and another pair of pots hold standardised ficus. The edge is treated with a neat row of box and the lattice is screened with compact lilypillies and cypress.

Seanna McCune's garden, NSW, Australia

Above: A bath gets another life in this courtyard, with its filling of water plants, native fish and tadpoles in the dappled shade of an old spreading gardenia. Standing in their pot in the water is a generous clump of water iris, *Iris pseudacorus*, its yellow flowers emerging in spring. Large leaves of a calathea drape across in front, a cane-stemmed begonia flowers behind, a treefern and busy lizzie dress the side with a silver-leafed plectranthus on the ground.

Pools that are set into the ground or built above it have become a lot easier and less troublesome with the development of waterproof membranes. Once the shape is established, it is lined with sand so the surface is smooth, the membrane is draped in, and generously taken up and over the sides. This prevents trickles escaping around the edges. It is essential not to pierce the membrane surface. Rocks or paving will conceal the overhanging liner, which can be trimmed to fit after the rocks are in position. The membrane can be concreted over and tiled or surfaced with rocks, or simply filled with water as it is. The dark lining gives the water a good reflective surface.

Just a shallow depression in a shaded corner, lined, rock edged and planted around can become a frog heaven with tadpoles eating mosquito larvae and the sound of gentle glomping calls marking your wildlife refuge. For more wildlife in your courtyard and even on a deck, place a heavy terracotta saucer or bowl with a rim for them to stand on, and birds will come to drink and bathe. Water can also be contained in a rejected bath filled with native fish, water plants and pots of iris, and secluded in a leafy corner. The sound of moving water can be cooling and soothing, whether it's an artful trickle tucked away discreetly, or the main event.

Bowls, fountains and pumps are all available at nurseries and landscaping supply stores. How to keep the water free of mosquitoes? Fish or tadpoles will feed on the larvae but the water must be deep and cool enough for the fish to survive. In shade or semi-shade, 30 to 35cm will suffice, but in sun the pool will have to be 40 to 50cm deep at least. Too shallow a pool in strong sunlight will also develop a dense algal growth. Fish may need protection from fishing birds. Pools without fish can be mosquito-proofed with regular sprayings of pyrethrum.

a feature wall

Here a blank brick wall has been converted to become the feature of this small courtyard. A trough planter only 50cm wide and 1m high was constructed against the wall with a central rectangle divided off. An extra lining of bricks was added at the back, the pool lined with waterproofing membrane and an additional course of bricks at the top neatly secures and obscures the membrane edge. The planter troughs have the same membrane protecting the back wall and an agricultural pipe drains the base and slopes to an outlet at the side. Gravel covers the drainage pipe to keep it clear of the potting mix on top of it. The wall and the trough were bagged and surfaced with lime wash to match the colour of the plaque. Water, pipes and a pump for the lion's head

water spout are fitted behind the wall. The troughs are planted symmetrically with plants for sunny conditions. Bright Marumi cumquats, *Fortunella japonica,* are laden with fruit in winter and are glossy-leafed all year. They will eventually have to be removed as their roots develop too generously for the site. They can be replaced exactly or with something different for a new look. The lavender used here is the almost continually flowering *Lavandula dentata,* often called French lavender. It needs frequent trimming of deadheads and leggy growth to develop a half-round, flowering shape to suit here. Apply slow-release fertiliser to the potting mix in spring and late summer to keep them all growing well and an occasional wash with liquid fertiliser on the cumquat leaves for green and lush growth. The lavenders can cope with little water once

settled in but the cumquats will need more. Give the troughs a good soaking once a week so the water travels down through the soil to the cumquat roots. In very hot dry conditions watch for any signs of wilting and top up the troughs to remedy.

ASPECT At least half a day's sun; can be west-facing

CLIMATE Mediterranean, temperate or subtropical

WATER Soak well once a week, watch for signs of drying out and give extra

EQUIPMENT Pump, piping, plaque with spout, pool liner, power, water

Mistilis garden, NSW, Australia

running over

Here a shallow square tiled pond is kept crystal clear by the pump and filter as the water fills and flows from the urn. Simply delightful, and dressed only by the fallen blossom of potato vine, *Solanum jasminoides,* and a treefern, *Dicksonia antarctica,* behind. In spring star jasmine, *Trachelospermum jasminoides,* the other twiner there, will scent the air and drop into the pool. Perhaps coloured leaves float there in autumn. The pump is in the urn and the pipe is fitted through the base.

ASPECT Semi-shade

CLIMATE Mediterranean, subtropical or temperate

EQUIPMENT A tiled pool or a square of pool liner, a tilted urn or bowl, pump, piping, power and water

marginal plants

Sweet flag, *Acorus calamus* 'Variegatus'. Cream-edged sword-like scented foliage with pink flush in spring. Sun.

Water plantain, *Alisma plantago-aquatica*. Deciduous in cool climates, oval leaves stand above water. Hazed with white flowers up to 1m tall in summer. Sun or semi-shade.

Flowering rush, *Butomus umbellatus*. Deciduous in cool areas, strappy narrow leaves, small massed pink flower heads on long stems in summer. Sun.

Papyrus, *Cyperus papyrus*. Tall stems to 1.5m, ball of leaves on top. Dwarf form suits small sites. Sun.

***Houttuynia cordata*.** Deciduous mounding groundcover, 'Chamaeleon' marbled pink and cream. Confine to a pot as it can become invasive. More colour variegation in sun.

Japanese iris, *Iris ensata*. Leaves up to 1m high, many colours available, flowers in spring. Can stand in the pond but remove from water in winter in cool areas. Part shade.

Louisiana iris, *Iris fulva*. Prefers warmer zones where it can remain in water through winter. Coppery flowers in spring. Semi-shade or sun. Many cultivars.

Yellow flag, *Iris pseudacorus*. Plain green or variegated foliage forms, spring flowers, likes edge or in pond placement. Sun or semi-shade.

Mat rush, *Lomandra longifolia* or *L. hystrix*. Dark green ribbon foliage, large clump, scented swords of flowers in spring. Sun or shade.

Nardoo, *Marsilea* spp. Clover-like leaves float on the surface. Sun.

New Zealand flax, *Phormium tenax*. Strappy erect foliage, various colours, large and dwarf forms available.

Bulrush, *Typha latifolia*. Tall strappy plant with stately dark brown seed heads. Invasive. Sun.

Sculptor: Chris Bennets, NSW; Designer: Katisma, NSW, Australia

plants for a water garden

Success with pond plants depends on selecting the right plants for the conditions they are to grow in, and on the depth of the pond. A shallow pond edge sinking to a deeper centre will allow the combination of bogside margin plants with those that must grow underwater. It is a more effective display in a small space if a maximum of three contrasting varieties are combined. Several of the same plant will look more natural and make a good impact. If combining plants, use an upright shape like iris, with a floating leaf variety like water lily, for contrast. If fish are planned for the pond, a cover of surface greenery will provide them with protection, but remove at least one-third of the cover regularly to prevent overcrowding and rotting of the plants. Pond waste is an excellent mulch on pots.

Marginal plants can be planted in constantly wet soil outside the pond or placed in their pots on ledges at the side. If the pond is too deep, put them on raised platforms of brick or upturned terracotta pots. Make sure the water level obscures the pot rim. Waterlilies and lotus pots should be more the 30cm below the surface. Proprietary pellets of fertiliser or clay-wrapped slow-release fertiliser can be pushed into the potting mix with the original planting and then reapplied each spring. Weigh the potting mix down with pebbles so it won't float out into the water. The extra weight will keep the pots upright. Repot and divide them every two years. Where winters are very cold, lift the pots out in autumn and store away from frost. If using a glazed or tiled pond in these conditions, float a block of wood on the surface to prevent the ice from cracking the container.

water and rocks

A rocky outcrop, carved granite bowl and pebbled surrounds have been set in a depression waterproofed with pool liner as an entry focus. The water is pumped from the lower rock-filled container into the bowl, the inlet obscured by strategically placed pebbles. The water gurgles and the damp rocks gleam. Madonna lilies in mild climates, plantain lilies in cooler zones leaf out the surrounds. Ferns would also appreciate the site. A white rose attends the entry, repeating the white forms of the pebbles.

ASPECT Sun or partial shade

CLIMATE Mediterranean, temperate or subtropical

EQUIPMENT Carved granite bowl, assorted sized and coloured river stones, pump, piping, power, water

making a small water feature

1. Select a waterproof bowl at least 30cm deep. Or plug the hole of a glazed pot with a plastic bung or piece of dowel. Fill with silicone sealant and press a square of heavy plastic over it. Seal the edges with more silicone and allow to dry before filling with water.

2. Select potted plants that are the right size for the container, so their rims will be obscured by the water surface. Also select a variety of leaf forms and/or heights for contrast. It may be necessary to stand some on bricks or pebbles to bring them up to the right height.

in-pond plants

Water poppy, *Hydrocleys nymphoides*. Floating oval leaves, poppy-like yellow flowers in summer. Best in warm zones in sun.

Sacred lotus, *Nelumbo nucifera*. Plant deeply in warm climates, blue-green large round leaves, tall flowers in several colour varieties in summer. Seed pods interesting. Deciduous. Sun-loving.

Brandy bottle lily, *Nuphar lutea*. Round leaves, die back in winter, small yellow flowers in summer. Cool zones in sun.

Water lilies, *Nymphaea* spp. There are some to suit cool areas, others for warmer. Colourings numerous. Sun and still water.

Fringed water lily, *Nymphoides* spp. Leaves like water lilies. Small fringed white flowers, *N. indica*, for warm zones, yellow *N. peltata* in cool. Sun.

Golden club, *Orontium aquaticum*. Clustered upright leaves, deciduous in cool zones, club-like yellow and white spikes stand from the foliage. Sun.

floating plants

Water fern, *Azolla* spp. Blue-green in shade, purplish in sun, crinkled foliage, can die back in cool zones.

Hydrocharis dubia. Floating pointed small waterlily-like leaves, white flowers. Deciduous in cool. Sun.

Duckweed, *Spirodela* spp or *Lemna* spp. Tiny bright green leaf-like structures float on the surface.

3. Place in position and fill the bowl with water. Place pebbles on the soil surface if necessary to stabilise pots. Add duckweed or water fern for surface cover if floating-leafed plants were not selected.

topiary

Topiary, the art of growing and trimming trees to a desired shape, is delightfully applicable to potted plants. A single shapely and well-maintained specimen has great formality and style. Paired, or lined up, they can mark an entry, soften a wall or frame a view. And they can be moved around as need arises or conditions change. Usually selected are slow-growing trees or shrubs, chosen so that constant trimming will not be necessary.

Growing and shaping them to a reasonable size takes some years so they are expensive to buy as mature, well shaped specimens, but well worth it if you require an instant effect. However, to maintain their shape and healthy leaf growth do not neglect them. Rough up the top surface of the soil and add an extra layer of potting mix no deeper than 2.5cm and feed them in spring and early autumn with slow-release fertiliser. Water this in well. If possible, keep them on pot feet to guarantee drainage, and soak the soil well once a week. Splash water over the leaves to wash them if rain does not reach them or if conditions are very dry. Plants must be able to absorb carbon dioxide and release oxygen and water vapour through their leaves to survive.

Maintaining the shaping of a prepared topiary involves vigilance. They usually have two growth spurts a year, but will occasionally burst forth when conditions change. Trim the new growth from the tree as it reaches beyond the prepared shape. New growth comes from the buds in the leaf/stem connection and will soon cover twiggy ends. Don't trim in too deeply and don't allow the twigs to get too woody or you'll have

Trim off soft new twigs to a leaf junction with your fingers if you want to be very precise, but use scissors or shears if there are lots to do.

unsightly holes until new growth appears. For round shaping, keep turning the pot and assessing with your eye. Shaping a tree is a constant but relaxing and creative garden art and allows people with limited mobility, little time or only a tiny site to still feel involved with gardening.

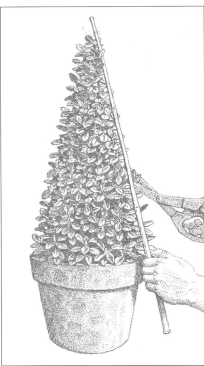

If straight shaping is required, the most accurate method is to use a cane leant against the tree or pot as a guide.

Left: A selection of neatly shaped and potted topiary ready for purchase — lilypilly and both English and Japanese box. It takes time for a slow-growing shrub to develop a trunk, and for shaping to be established, so such purchases are always expensive. However, the instant effect is excellent. They will all need constant care with watering, feeding and at least twice-yearly trimming to maintain their manicured good looks.

Photo: Gil Hanly Gina Williamson's garden, N.Z.

a courtyard cluster

Left: This collection of four pots displays how well topiary can emphasise and dress a corner, prettily now in a sea of new spring green, dramatically in winter surrounded by leafless Japanese maples. The tall spiral at the back, English box, *Buxus sempervirons*, is nicely balanced with a pair of double mop-headed Japanese box, *Buxus microphylla*. In front is a round ball of *Buxus sempervirons*, 'Aureo variegata', making a nice contrast. Mondo grass in two pots links with the edging around the garden, planted with more green of stinking hellebore and a pot of a libertia. All of these plants are happy in shady sites.

ASPECT Partial shade

CLIMATE All but tropical

WATER Soak once a week

POT SIZE Assorted

PLANTS 1 English box, 2 Japanese box, 1 *Buxus sempervirons*

archway sentinels

This shapely pair of *Juniperus chinensis* 'Kaisuka' grow symmetrically but individually from their terracotta pots. Occasional side branches have been removed revealing the red-brown bark. Those that remain have been trimmed short and club-like in a casual arrangement up the stem. The trunks have been given twists by weighting them to bend one way, then letting them return to straight, then weighting in another direction as they grow. The process takes some years but the effect is worth the effort. The orbs require trimming twice or three times a year and further upward growth is now stopped as the leader has been trimmed.

ASPECT Full sun

CLIMATE All but tropical

WATER Soak well once a week

POT SIZE 30-50cm

PLANTS 2 *Juniperus chinensis* 'Kaisuka'

Photo: Gil Hanly Designed by John Burton Topiary, Te Puna, Tauranga, NZ.

It is possible to grow and shape your own topiary as long as you are patient. Buy as big a specimen as your budget will allow, bearing in mind the shape you plan to make and the site it is to fill: shady, bright sun or wind-buffeted. Repot into a heavy cast stone, terracotta or concrete pot just a size or two bigger than the existing pot if it is to go on show straight away, otherwise continue with plastic to save on expense and to make moving easier.

Make early side trimmings of stems then leaves on the trunk if standardising, but allow the tip to reach full height before it is trimmed. Regular trimming of the ball on top will make it dense and round. Form a double or triple mop head by leaving the side shoots in appropriate spaces on the trunk, but continually trim their stem ends. To form a ball without a trunk, remove the growing tip as soon as the plant is the right height and keep shaping all growth into a round. A cone is made by

trimming off side shoots tapering from the base, which should be left as wide as the pot, to the growing tip, but do not trim this until the plant has reached the desired height. You can also indulge in elaborate shaping like spirals and animals.

Why not try a deciduous variety? A ball of twigs could look interesting in winter. Standardising is also possible with many fast-growing shrubs or vines. Once they have grown a length of trunk that can be supported by a stake, they make very effective topiary shapes. Sometimes several plants can be positioned close together and their trunks plaited as they grow. The trunks are kept clear of side shoots and a good mop head develops. Sometimes grafted varieties can be bought with a stout trunk and weeping or bunching crowns that can be shaped. See what is available and what is recommended at your nursery.

Use the same techniques to shape and maintain as is described above. Do remember to trim them fairly hard

immediately after flowering and possibly again in three and six months, to maintain the shape. Try duranta in its white- or blue-flowered forms, acalypha, murraya, cistus, robinia, viburnum, potato vine or wisteria to name a few.

Plants suitable for trimming and shaping are usually evergreen shrubs or trees with smallish leaves

Banksia, *Banksia integrifolia*

Box, all *Buxus* varieties

Camellia, *Camellia sasanqua*

Conifers, dense varieties like *thuja, chamaecyparis,* juniper, cypress, yew

Cotoneaster varieties

Weeping fig, *Ficus benjamina*

Privet, *Ligustrum ovalifolium, Lonicera nitida*

Bay, *Myrtus communis*

Serissa foetida, there is a variegated form also; leaves smell when cut or bruised

Lilypilly, *Syzygium* spp, compact varieties

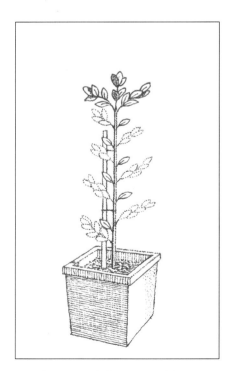

To make a topiary ball, once a trunk has developed, trim off alternate side branches.

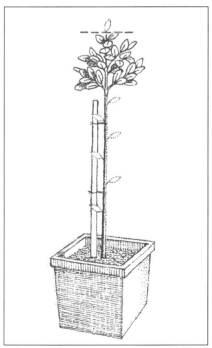

Cut off the leader when it has reached the right height and remove all the side shoots.

In time and with constant trimming, the leafy top will fill out.

1. Early stages of vine topiary growth with the wire frame being inserted over the centrally placed plant, in this case, a muehlenbeckia or maiden hair vine.

Pictured at Elegant Outdoors, NSW, Australia

Above: This attractive and quickly filled ring of star jasmine is an example of a speedy 'topiary' effect. Select a plant with at least two leggy stems and position in the pot with a wire form inserted. Secure the stems to both sides of the shape. As they grow, train them around the shape. Every so often, nip the top 3cm from the growing stems to encourage new lateral stems to shoot. It will thicken as it grows and will achieve this effect in a year.

2. The wiry stems are woven into the frame. With constant twining of new growth and trimming of stem ends to encourage branching, it will cover the frame in a year.

And simpler still are small-leafed vines like ivy, creeping fig and muehlenbeckia which can be planted around or under a moulded orb or animal shape frame and twisted to climb into and conceal it as it grows. Circle and heart shapes are also available, around which can be trained vines like potato vine, star jasmine, Carolina jasmine, true jasmines, honeysuckle, hoya or black-eyed Susan. Most vigorous twining climbers will fill the circle in a year and make attractive and long-lasting pot plants. Another alternative for a great effect is to pack the centre of the mould with sphagnum moss and tuck or wire into it clumping succulents like mother-of-pearl plant, moonstones or house leeks. All of these need very little watering.

bonsai

The classical art of bonsai has travelled through time from its origins in China as 'penjing' over 2000 years ago, to Japan 1000 years later, but was not seen outside Japan or China until 100 years ago. It quickly became popular in the West as people saw the beauty in form and detail of miniature trees. Even though bonsai are garden specimens, they can be brought indoors for short periods to use as a display. One of the earliest uses of bonsai was to bring inside small apricot trees in bloom in late winter as perfumed harbingers of spring.

The art of bonsai — being able to create scenes and shapes to imitate nature — is another reason for its appeal. There are many suppliers of bonsai specimens (it's always safest to buy from a reputable grower), they make delightful gifts and are a joy to own. However maintaining them does require some special care. They are garden pot plants, needing light, air and frequent watering or rain to keep them at their best, growing vigorously in a tiny pot of soil. The technique of pruning their roots stimulates their redevelopment and their capacity to absorb nutrients and water from the potting mix.

Repotting and retrimming of their roots is done every two or three years.

Below: Beautifully shaped to cascade out of a tall pot, this conifer is an excellent example of styling. The stem has been pruned and wired over many years to establish this form.

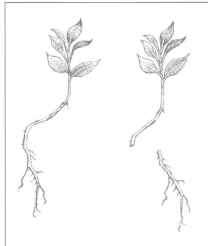

Select a seedling with a thickened trunk. Cut the root section in half and repot. You can pot the lower root also, as it will often reshoot.

The following year, trim off the longest sections of roots and start to trim branches.

Megumi Bennett, Bonsai Art, NSW, Australia

Spring is the best time for this, giving the plant time to develop new roots and new growth before summer.

Setting up your own bonsai is not difficult, but it does take some time. Select a seedling tree or shrub, preferably with some thickening to its trunk, cut its primary root in half and return the plant to the pot. Three to six months later, preferably in spring or autumn, trim off the longest sections of the newly developed secondary roots.

At the same time assess the shape and potential of the trunk and stem development and thin out branches from the trunk to develop the aged tree appearance. In two or three years, root-prune again and continue shaping the trunk. Techniques and styles of shaping cannot be covered here, but help is available in books and classes should you wish to learn more.

plants suitable for bonsai

Maples, particularly Japanese and trident

Other autumn-colouring trees like Chinese tallow, oak, beech, English hawthorn, liquidambar, ginkgo, dogwood and elm

Fruiting trees like pears, quince, cherry, crabapple, apple, cotoneaster, lime, cumquat or peach

Conifers like pines, cypress, junipers and spruce

Small-leafed camellias or azaleas

Native trees like banksia, blueberry ash, figs, Illawarra flame tree, and Queensland bottle tree

Right: This *Ficus deltoidea*, or mistletoe fig, is 18 years old. As a bushy shrub it would grow to 2 metres high and wide but constrained by bonsai, it becomes a miniatured replica. The berries ripen to yellow and decorate the bush for a long time.

Polly Park garden, Canberra, Australia

Above: A Japanese maple beautifully shaped and displayed in a fence 'window'. The moss groundcover is traditional and evidence of the essential frequent watering regime required by bonsai. The bamboo hedge behind adds more flavour of the orient.

Megumi Bennett, Bonsai Art, NSW, Australia

cacti

Cacti and succulents are a special group of plants that have adapted to survive a harsh life. They will survive without water for very long periods, endure wind battering, savage sun and near freezing night temperatures and yet produce delicate silky flowers, some tiny but others quite large, often mysteriously opening at night. The intricate patterning of cacti spines, ribs, shapes and markings makes for an astounding variety.

The survival equipment of cacti includes the absence of leaves, thus reducing water loss, an ability to store water in expanding cells, toughened skin to resist the sun and the cold,

shaping that will allow wind to blow about them but flow over them, and spines, bristles or hairs to protect them from predators.

Handle cacti with care, even those that don't appear armed. Spines in the fingers can be very difficult to remove and can be a great irritation.

Succulents, the un-spiny relations, have made similar adjustments for survival and are just as showy and varied. They all require very grainy fast-draining soil and will rot if left soaking in water or continually damp soil. Cactus mix is available at most nurseries or can be mixed at home with equal quantities of coarse sand and good quality potting mix. Add a couple of handfuls of small-grade

pebbles. The root system is not extensive so they can be planted in relatively small pots. Large specimens make more impact but are, of course, more expensive. However, grouping or mass planting smaller specimens looks effective.

Always crock the pots well and stand them on pot feet or at least fast-drying tiles or slate, not wood. Water them only occasionally in summer and even more sparingly during winter or while resting after flowering. Most will not survive frost as the expanded frozen water breaks the cells where it is stored. To protect them, move plants to a bright position under cover inside and you'll be rewarded with winter flowers.

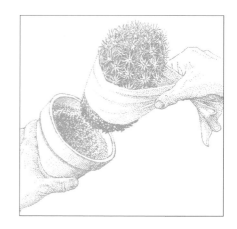

Lift the cactus with a cloth or paper tightly wound around the plant and extending beyond it to become a handle.

colour-coded container

This delightful arrangement includes the pot and floor decoration and a superbly suitable succulent, *Echeveria* 'Topsy Turvy', here adorned with its winter flowers. Take in if frost is likely and bring out for daily sun baths, or in milder conditions leave it in full sun for maximum leaf colouration. Trim off the spent flower heads but leave it alone for a month or two after flowering. Trim off overcrowded and leggy growth that will destabilise the pot. The trimmings will grow when pushed into cactus mix.

a clutch of cacti

Baking happily in full sun on heat-absorbing black slate is a group of prickly cacti and structural succulents. Although they don't lean about and entwine with their neighbours as many clustered plants do, they certainly make their mark by standing rigidly to attention in their pots, displaying their intricate and varied patterning and colourings with what appears to be pride. They almost have their arms folded, chins and chests out and a challenge in their stance. And why not? They can survive almost anywhere and look good while they're at it. Often decorative gravel is placed over the mix, helping to hold it in wind, and enhancing their desert-like appearance. When choosing plants, remember to select differing heights, textures, shapes and colours in the cacti, with a couple of succulents for a real contrast.

ALL CACTI AND SUCCULENTS

ASPECT Full sun

CLIMATE Mediterranean, temperate (moving indoors for freezing conditions), and subtropical

WATER Water lightly only during warm months

cacti courtyard

This welled courtyard has great drama with a stunning arrangement of rugged cacti and structural succulents, some positioned in light soil cover among the rocks, others in pots. Large stone slabs dress the site and support some of the pots among the pebble mulch. Tall spiky cacti are assorted forms of cereus with a wonderfully gnarled *C. peruvianus* 'Monstrosus' in the centre. In the pot on high sits a golden barrel cactus *Echinacactus grusonii* and below is a grass-like *Agave stricta* looking in need of a feed or water. These are filled out with a many-fingered *Euphorbia tirucallii* in front of a tall *Yucca aloifolia*. Several spiky aloes and shrubby crassulas complete the scene.

bulbs in pots

Growing bulbs in pots makes possible a great moveable display. They are the traditional harbinger of spring, but there are also varieties that can see you through the year in most climates, creating an additional highlight in summer, autumn and winter for your potted display. Another benefit of growing bulbs in pots is that it allows you to grow many more than would normally grow in your garden because you are able to control soil, climate and light requirements for each pot. Move them out of vision when they start to look dismal as leaves die down or, if evergreen, move them into the background.

Bulbs must have good drainage so use good-quality potting mix and do not add any extra peat or moisture-holding material. Bulbs will rot if they lie in water so make sure the pots have adequate open drainage holes, and spread a generous layer of pebbles, gravel or crocks on the bottom. Stand them on pot feet or a freely-draining surface. Make sure the pot you select is the right size for the fully grown bulbs. Bulbs grown in pots are not planted as deeply as in the garden, their tips are usually placed about 1cm below the rim of the pot, so add sufficient potting mix to allow the bulbs to be positioned at the appropriate level. Line up the

bulbs on this surface, massed for a good display but not touching each other. Keep them clear of the sides of the pot as this can become too hot for them. Fill the pot with extra potting mix and shake it to settle the soil. Water to dampen. If the potting mix does not contain slow-release fertiliser, add it as you plant; apply weak solutions of liquid fertiliser once a month as leaves start to show through, and continue until they fade, to nourish the bulb for next year's blooming. Let evergreen bulbs rest after flowering but apply slow-release fertiliser every six months.

Right: In an aged pot that has been concreted for stability onto the stone wall, stands a pot of 'Dove Wings' daffodils. The petals on this form of daffodil fold back, dove-like, and the trumpet is narrow.

Below: A delightful mix of marmalade-coloured tulips and violas looks sunny even on grey days. Plant tulips in late autumn or early winter as the soil starts to cool, positioning them so bulb tips are just below the surface, 6 to 8cm apart. As soon as the leaves break through, add established viola seedlings in the spaces between. Cut the tulip flowers as they finish and the violas will romp and hide the fading tulip leaves.

Above: White bells with a green-spotted rim are obliging snowflakes, *Leucojum vernum*, standing tall above rich green leaves. They can be left for years to fill a pot, fed with slow-release fertiliser as spikes emerge and richly mulched once leaves die. When too crowded, divide the clumps while bulbs are dormant.

potted bulbs in flower for spring

temperate zones
Anemone nemorosa (windflower)

Crocus flavus; *Crocus vernus*

Erythronium 'Pagoda' (dog tooth violet)

Galanthus spp (snow drop)

Hyacinthus orientalis (hyacinth)

Ipheion varieties (spring star flower)

Iris, bulbous

Ixia (corn lily)

Leucojum vernum (snowflake)

Muscari varieties (grape hyacinth)

Narcissus (daffodils and jonquils)

Puschkinia scilloide

Scilla siberica (Siberian squill)

Tulipa varieties (tulips)

mediterranean zones
Anemone blanda (Greek windflower)

Babiana stricta (Baboon flower)

Freesia hybrids

Hippeastrum

Hyacinth

Ipheion (spring star flower)

Ixia (corn lily)

Lachenalia (soldier boy)

Muscari varieties (grape hyacinth)

Sparaxis varieties (harlequin flower)

Leucocoryne ixiodes (glory of the sun)

Narcissus (daffodils and jonquils)

Scilla (bluebells)

Tulipa varieties (tulips)

subtropical zones
Babiana stricta (Baboon flower)

Eucharis amazonica (Eucharist lily)

Freesia

Hyacinth

Hippeastrum

Ipheion (spring star flower)

Ixia (corn lily)

Lachenalia (soldier boy)

Muscari (grape hyacinth)

Narcissus (daffodils and jonquils)

Rhodophiala chilense (hippeastrum)

Scadoxus puniceus (paint brush)

Scilla varieties (bluebell)

Sparaxis varieties (harlequin flower)

Sprekelia formosissima (Jacobean lily).

Tulipa varieties (tulips)

Zantedeschia (calla lily)

tropical zones
Eucharis amazonica (Eucharist lily)

Hippeastrum

Rhodophiala chilense

Sandersonia aurantiaca (Christmas bells)

Scadoxus puniceus (paint brush).

Wurmbea spicata

Zantedeschia (calla lily)

potted bulbs in flower for summer

temperate zones
Allium varieties (ornamental onion)
Begonia varieties (tuberous begonia)
Crinum x *powellii* (crinum)
Dahlia hybrids
Lilium varieties
Nomocharis mairei
Tropaeolum speciosum (climbing nasturtium)

mediterranean zones
Achimenes varieties (hot water plant)
Allium varieties (ornamental onion)
Canna varieties
Crinum varieties

Dahlia
Gloriosa superba (gloriosa vine)
Habranthus varieties
Lilium varieties
Moraea polystachya (peacock iris)
Tigridia pavonia (jockeys cap lily)

subtropical zones
Achimenes varieties (hot water plant)
Caladium
Canna varieties
Crinum varieties
Crytanthus varieties (vallota or Scarborough lily)
Dahlia
Gloriosa superba
Habranthus varieties
Hymenocallis littoralis (spider lily)

Lilium varieties
Moraea polystacha (peacock iris)
Tigridia pavonia (jockeys cap lily)
Worsleya rayneri (blue amaryllis)

tropical zones
Achimenes varieties (hot water plant)
Canna varieties
Cyrtanthus varieties (vallota or Scarborough lily)
Gloriosa superba
Habranthus varieties
Hymenocallis littoralis (spider lily)
Proiphys amboinensis (Cardwell lily)
Worsleya rayneri (blue amaryllis)

potted bulbs in flower for autumn

temperate zones
Amaryllis belladonna (naked lady)
Cyclamen.
Leucojum autumnale
Lycoris incarnata and *L. squamigera* (spider lily)
Nerine bowdenii (Guernsey lily)
Sternbergia varieties (autumn crocus)

mediterranean zones
Amaryllis belladonna (naked lady)
Leucojum vernum (snowflake)
Lycoris varieties (spider lily)
Nerine varieties (Guernsey lily)
Sternbergia varieties (autumn crocus)
Zephyranthes (rain lily)

subtropical zones
Amaryllis belladonna (naked lady)
Leucojum vernum (snowflake)
Lycoris varieties (spider lily)
Nerine varieties (Guernsey lily)
Zephyranthes varieties (rain lily)

tropical zones
Caladium varieties (angel wings)
Eucharis grandiflora (Eucharist lily)
Pamianthe peruviana

Designer: Michael Cooke, NSW, Australia

Left: The Empress of Brazil, or blue amaryllis, *Worsleya rayneri*, is a bulb for tropical and subtropical garden displays but it can be grown in a hot house in cold conditions. It demands warmth all year and humidity, particularly during summer, in free-draining but rich potting mix. The lushly-leafed stems produce flower spikes in late spring or summer.

Left: Winter daffodils always look cheerful. Well-developed bulbs will produce several flowers which will open in full sunlight over at least a month. Pick off finished blooms so energy is not wasted on seed production. Let the leaves die down naturally to nourish the bulbs for next year. Ipheion, spring star flowers, are just starting in the other pot.

potted bulbs in flower for winter

temperate zones
Cyclamen
Narcissus varieties (daffodils and jonquils)

mediterranean zones
Cyclamen
Geissorhiza varieties (wine cup)
Narcissus varieties (jonquils and daffodils)
Polyxena varieties

subtropical zones
Clivea miniata (clivea)
Cyclamen
Geissorhiza varieties (wine cup)
Leucojum vernum (snowflake)
Narcissus varieties (daffodils and jonquils)
Polyxena varieties

tropical zones
Eucharis grandiflora

Below: A trough of white cyclamen with their decorative marbled leaves makes an attractive show throughout the cold winter months. Variegated ivy has been added to drape over the trough. As the cyclamen leaves die off, summer flowering annuals can be added. Apply slow-release fertiliser as cyclamen leaves start to shoot and as they finish, to maintain the vitality of the potting mix. Top dress with compost.

Photo: Gil Hanly

Above: These three cymbidium pots have been brought to the sunlit centre of this courtyard under a still leafless tree in late winter. Some of the flower spikes are still opening, promising extended colour, but the massed display is delightful. Added for variety is a splendid orange clivea and a purple-leafed plant the owners were told was a Natal plum, *Carissa horizontalis*.

orchids

Don't let the vision of delicate and sculptured orchids frighten you off growing them. Mostly they are resilient plants growing naturally on trees or rocks and the tiny crevices between them, or on the forest floor. The key to success is to start with the right orchid that will suit your environment. Most orchids like shade, some requiring more than others.

For semi-shaded conditions with some hours of sunlight in mild temperate, Mediterranean and subtropical zones try Cymbidiums. Where the chance of freezing is possible they can be moved under cover for protection, but they must have cool nights to stimulate flower production. Their rich fans of strappy leaves are evergreen, the flower spikes emerging from the base of the pseudobulb during autumn or early winter and growing easily 60cm tall. They can have up to 30 flowers per spike and there can be many spikes in a well-massed pot. Flowers, as they open in winter or early spring, will last a couple of months. Many colours are available and there are miniature as well as standard forms to select. To keep them growing well, cut off the flower spikes before they shrivel, using some in their prime in vases indoors. After flowering allow the plants to rest for about a month and just moisten the pseudobulbs. Then top up the pot with extra orchid potting mix (see page 13), re-commence watering, allowing the potting mix to dry between wettings, and feed them with nitrogen-rich

Left: Still looking magnificent a month later, the orchids are now screened and the show enriched by the delicate froth of plum blossom overhead. The shade of the leaf-filled tree will be sufficient for their summer protection.

liquid fertiliser every two weeks during summer, or use slow-release pellets. Apply flower-inducing fertiliser with extra phosphorus as autumn approaches.

Smaller orchids for similar conditions are the dendrobiums. These plants grow naturally on rock or trees, their meagre roots holding them in position and their stem-like pseudobulbs storing water and nutrients. The varieties from trees are often purchased attached to bark or pieces of wood, and look delightful displayed on a wall or among branches of a tree. They will survive well if watered gently but frequently, as the water drains away fast, and splashed with liquid fertiliser every month to simulate the nutrients available from decomposing vegetation from trees. The rock-growing orchids are more usually sold in pots and will grow there well in free-draining orchid potting mix and treated as above. They mostly flower in late winter/spring, and their colours and forms are numerous, some minute, some extravagant and some perfumed. Many suit basket growth.

Jack Hiles' garden, NSW, Australia

Photo: Andre Martin

Above: A stunning cascade of *Cymbidium lowianum*, is actually growing in the crutch of a tree. Any of the cymbidiums and dendrobiums would do similarly. It is watered frequently when the rain doesn't come, and fed with liquid fertiliser every month. It is protected by a hill from hot westerly sun and lightly shaded by the tree in this subtropical climate. Its owner is justifiably proud.

Left: True to its common name, the rock orchid can grow happily on rocks with a build-up of decaying leaf matter to sustain it. It will also adjust to life in a pot, supported in large-particled orchid potting mix. The great branches of flowers emerge slowly as well-wrapped spikes in the centre of each leaf cluster through autumn and winter, opening in spring.

73

Where you have a few hours of sunlight during winter try oncidiums. They produce delicate sprays of bright blooms from a leafy stem in winter or early spring. 'Dancing ladies' orchid is a good example. Keep them just moist and their environs humid.

In intense shade in temperate, Mediterranean, subtropical and tropical zones, paphiopedilums, the slipper orchids are at their best. They have a remarkable slipper-like pouch in the centre, a waxy appearance and can last for months. Keep them just-moist always, well shaded and feed only once a month with weak liquid fertiliser. Break up the clump and repot generous divisions when the pot becomes overcrowded. The extravagant looking cattleyas, often used in corsages or wedding bunches, require more light than slipper orchids but need similar protection from burning midday sun.

In really tropical conditions where nights do not cool, grow vandas, phalaenopsis or Singapore orchids, or smaller sarcochilus varieties. They all like some protection from burning sun and require high humidity, regular watering and feeding and good drainage. Some of them suit hanging baskets.

There are many more varieties of orchid; if you have difficulty in growing them, try a generous pot of crucifix orchid, *Epidendrum ibaguense*. They will thrive in full sun or semi-shade, as long as you keep them in a free-draining potting mix.

Right: Reaching well above its foliage stands a neatly rounded and well-spotted slipper orchid. There are many varieties, shapes and colours available but all have their trade mark 'slipper' pouch in the centre. A fascinating splash of the exotic in winter for well-shaded sites.

Right: Two dendrobiums on a tree, one nestled into the fork, the other attached originally with twine but now clinging. This perfect site ensures summer shade, autumn dappled light with leaf thinning and eventual drop in late winter. Flowers of the orchids will scent the air in spring.

gardens in the air

Lifting plants from ground level to a position on a window ledge, a wall or hanging from a beam can give height and fullness to a potted display. It will also give you more space to grow things, it allows you to specifically place plants so they can reach extra sun or increased shade as required, and it can be used to screen out eyesores or provide privacy. There are infinite combinations to try and many containers to suit the task.

hanging baskets

Choose a colour scheme to suit your needs, plants to suit your sunny or shady site, baskets in the right size to fill your space and arrangements to express your artistic ideals.

Above: A traditional ball of colour, this large wire basket has been lined with sphagnum moss and filled with an extravagant mix of colour and shapes of flowers and foliage. The aim when planning such a display is to select a variety of plants that will weave themselves together as they grow, will come into flower together and will continue to flower over a couple of months. Many of the classic choices have been made here. In the centre is a fuchsia, with purple and red colourings, standing nicely upright for height with its weeping blooms establishing the rounded shape. Just peeping over the top are the pink flowers of an ivy geranium, *Pelargonium peltatum*, often used in the same manner, for height and fall. Surrounding the fuchsia is the intense purple of lobelia, *Lobelia erinus*, with a white eye. Lobelias are very successful in hanging baskets as they climb to grow if supported, or mass and tumble in flowery cascades. Their colours include pink, blue, mauve and purple, pale to intense and a pure white contrast. The gentle daisy with fine filigree foliage is an Australian native plant now used around the world, *Brachyscome multifida*, 'Break o' Day'. Several plants wander through this cluster. Seaside daisy, *Erigeron karvinskianus* would also suit. Strong clumpings of colour come from three bedding begonias, *Begonia semperflorens*, a pink, a red and a white seen here. At least six would have been used altogether and true to their Latin name, are always in flower once started. More strong colour comes from busy lizzies, *Impatiens* cultivars, in nice compact new plant shapes. Tumbling leafy stems with white stars in the front is a bacopa which must have a moist position. Sweet Alice, *Lobularia maratima*, in all its colour tones could be a useful alternative in such a planting. Leafy contrasts are provided by several aluminium plant varieties, *Lamium* 'White Nancy', a yellow-leafed form and *L. purpureum*. Variegated ivy geraniums, small-leafed ivies, groundcovering ivy, *Glechoma hederacea* 'Variegata' or ornamental grape, *Ampelopsis brevipedunculata* 'Elegans' could substitute. A touch of grey is included with a dusty miller, *Centaurea cineraria*, although the round-leafed *Helichrysum petiolare* is more often used.

Left: Using a hanging pot with a flat base, this flowery mix is rich with buttery cream lit by mauve and purple contrasts. Cascading over the edges are cream compact nasturtiums, *Tropaeolum majus*. The mauve heads are a colour-matched selection of *Verbena* x *hybrida*. Both these and the seedling nasturtiums were alternated at 10cm intervals around the edge of the pot in good quality mix with added fertiliser. The centre was filled with a ring of purple petunias, again alternately planted with cream nasturtiums. The leafy bulk below holds them upright. Keep them well watered but don't give extra liquid fertiliser or you'll get all leaves and few flowers. Keep well trimmed to get bushy growth and remove dead flowers to encourage new ones.

Right: Softly cream and mauve with shouts of yellow, this round-based basket has been filled with a large assortment of plants. The bright yellow comes from a marigold hybrid, *Tagetes* 'Tangerine Gem', grown leggy to reach out of the mass, and more compact daisy-like *Senecio pectinatus*. Cream- and mauve-flowered petunias stand in the centre with a toning mauve *Scaevola* 'Mauve Clusters' generously draping from the edge. Sharing the centre is *Felicia* 'Mauve Cloud', its erect daisy flowers forming a halo effect. Planted in the base are mauve-toned *Lobelia erinus* and lime-green creeping jenny, *Lysimachia mummularia* 'Aurea'. Plant all these as seedlings in spring into potting mix with slow-realease fertiliser included, and water generously with liquid fertiliser each month. Trim off deadheads and leggy extensions to maintain the ball-of-flower effect throughout summer.

planting a hanging basket

When planting up a round ball display, stand the basket on a table or large pot to keep it steady as you work. If using sphagnum moss, dampen it and pack a good thick layer into the inside base of the basket. Press some moistened potting mix into that. From the outside, push through a hole with your finger and put the well-dampened roots of a trailing plant in the potting mix. Distribute three or four about the base. Plant them clear of the stabilising pot's edges so they won't be damaged as you work, or leave them till last if you're working on a table. Add more moss and more potting mix in layers, planting in as you go. Take the moss right to the top of the basket and position the tall plants in the centre. Top up with the final layer of potting mix.

Left: A sphagnum moss-lined basket just planted with petunias, geraniums and alyssum in the top and marigolds in the base. Established flowering plants were used.

Sprinkle on slow-release fertiliser if the potting mix does not contain it already. Don't be concerned that it looks a bit sparse in these early days, it will take at least a month to fill out. You can speed things up by using already flowering plants, but they will still need some time to meld. When using a moulded liner like coconut fibre, place it in the wire basket, dampen it and fill it with damp potting mix. Sprinkle over slow-release fertiliser if it's not already in the mix. Slit the liner with a knife in each place as you plant, opening up the fibre with your fingers. Push each plant's roots into the space and then press it all together again so mix will not spill out. Plant as above, trailing varieties at the base and around the edges, plants with stronger stems all about and the tallest ones in the centre on the top.

Left: Another newly planted basket, this one using established plants of petunia, marigolds, alyssum, lobelia, and parsley for leafy contrast.

For those solid bowls where plants cannot be inserted at the base, plant the trailers around the edge, and the tall ones in the centre. Give them a good watering to finish and hang them up to drip. Life will be a lot easier for the waterer if you have a long watering wand attached to the hose (or strap the hose firmly onto a length of dowel) to allow water to be directed into the centre of the basket. Always water generously and watch for signs of wilting. A drip watering system into the basket is ideal, computer-controlled if you tend to forget to turn it on. Hanging baskets of one plant only are as effective in their own way as these balls of colour. Often the cascading form of fuchsias, columnias, crab claw cactus, begonias or trailing geraniums or twisting arms of streptocarpus or hot water plant can make just as big an impact.

Left: Six weeks later the plants have established their patterns of growth and are starting to meld together. The petunias on top and lobelias below will need frequent tip pruning.

windowboxes

Window ledges are another space that can become the garden, especially appropriate in tiny city houses or small apartments. They are decorative, adding charm and softness to the view, from both inside and out. They can also be functional, with herbs and vegetables growing outside your kitchen window. Or a windowbox can be used to provide interest to what would otherwise be a dull view, or to screen it.

Lois Clarke's garden

Above: This hoya grows in a wooden windowbox with a wooden frame approximately the window size supporting it. A bar across the top and three-quarters of the way up provides stability and a link between the uprights. As the hoya grew, its stems were wired to the frame. It faces the morning sun and flowers non-stop through summer into autumn. It and the stained glass panel draw the eye to the window rather than the view beyond.

Above: Right on the street front in summer, this window ledge has been dressed with a wrought iron bracket holding a plastic trough. The lightness of plastic makes it very useful in a situation like this where lifting will be necessary, roots will not become too hot and water will not evaporate so readily. But do take care that it will be steady in winds and secured against vandals. Plants with minimal water demands are grouped here to great effect. The pink-flowered geranium is one of the slow-growing compact ivy-leaf cultivars that are just right for windowboxes. Many also have variegated foliage. Another suitable variety are the dwarf zonal types with coloured foliage like the purple-leafed 'Leonie Holborow' or the compact 'Fiat' series with well indented leaves. Keep nipping off the deadheads on the geraniums to encourage new flowering and trim off lanky stem growth

to maintain compactness. Trailing prettily through are several lobelias, *Lobelia erinus,* selected from a mixed colour punnet of seedlings. Thin the growth underneath lobelias to keep them delicate and prevent the build up of dead woody material. The wandering grey stems with almost circular leaves are *Helichrysum petiolare,* one of the best weaving foliage contrasts about. The yellow-leafed variety, 'Aureum', is also included. Trim off stems that wander too far to maintain compactness. They can grow all year in most climates but will eventually become too leggy and matted for a position like this. A couple of variegated periwinkles, *Vinca major* 'Variegata', have been planted at the back to provide some interest from inside as these shade-loving plants will not lean towards the light as the others do. All are planted in spring or early summer in good quality potting mix

containing slow-release fertiliser. Water well twice a week and more in very hot periods. Add liquid fertiliser to the mix once a month.

ASPECT At least half a day's full sun

CLIMATE Mediterranean, temperate and subtropical

WATER Twice a week

POT SIZE To fit window ledge securely

PLANTS 2 or 3 compact ivy-leaf geraniums, 6 lobelia, 2 grey-leafed helichrysum, 1 golden-leafed helichrysum, 3 variegated periwinkles. For a winter display try new plants of golden-leafed helichrysum with white primulas or yellow polyanthus; grey helichrysum with pink mixed primulas, or a row of gleaming kalanchoes.

Left: The focal point on this silvered deck garden is the planter box overflowing with colour. A bench behind is backed by the grey-green foliage of several plume poppies, *Macleaya cordata*, a perennial that grows up to 1.5m tall in summer, dying down in winter. Pinkish-grey plumes top the stems in summer. Filling the planter box are purple petunias, pink and purple trailing verbenas and wide spreading grey-leafed stems of *Helichrysum petiolare*. They will all benefit from regular nipping back of stem ends to keep up the flowering and control their spread. The surprise inclusion is an orange zinnia, *Zinnia angustifolia*. The planting could take on any colour combinations if a change seemed necessary — all white, yellow and white, red and orange, blue and white or blue and yellow — using these or any other trailing and flowering annual to suit. In very cool winters the box could be covered with a heavy top and become a table for bonsai or bulb pots. In milder winters the planting can be replaced by winter blooming varieties.

Right: Other boxed gardens can increase your garden space, provide a focal point or allow access to soil for those in wheelchairs and those with limited mobility. On a smoothly paved courtyard these beds have been built up with hardwood sleepers, designed to allow reachable access from all points, heavy enough to hold their position when stacked and large enough to allow them to be filled with good-quality garden soil. Drainage is provided by agricultural pipes at the base. Here a flourishing vegetable garden can be easily maintained, watered, manured, mulched and harvested as required.

Pictured at Ryde Horticultural College, NSW, Australia

espalier

Formal, space-saving, decorative, intriguing espalier is a delightful way to dress a wall. Shrubs or trees are pruned to grow in two dimensions only and are sometimes trained into a designed shape, often flat against a wall, but they can also be free-standing. The technique, though slow, can have many uses in a courtyard. They can be grown as a screen, their thinness but density taking up less space than a hedge in a confined area. They can be angled to catch the sun and become more effective fruit-, flower- and berry-producers. They can be shaped to frame a feature like a fountain or plaque or disguise a weakness. And they can decorate in a casual or controlled manner what might otherwise have been a blank wall. Before starting, you need to plan: the area to be covered, the shrubs or trees to suit both the site and conditions (formal, cottagey, sunny, shady, frosty, windy or humid), and then the shape and height that will give most effect. It's the leaf and growth shape of the chosen plants, the design of the shaping and density of cover required that will dictate how many plants are necessary. Some espalier patterns are shown here.

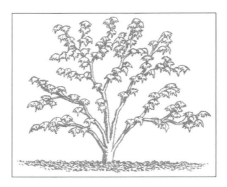

Free-form espalier with only branches at the back and front removed.

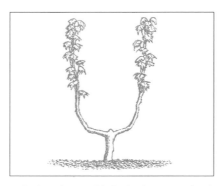

A single U shape, with the leader removed and a pair of branches trained upright.

To achieve this double cordon pattern, remove the leader and train the paired branches.

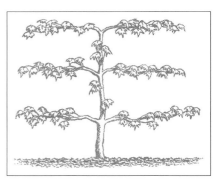

Triple horizontal cordon pattern. All but paired branches at regular intervals removed.

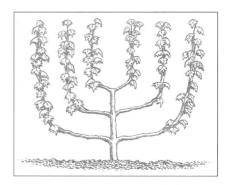

Palmette verrier pattern, established after several paired branches have developed.

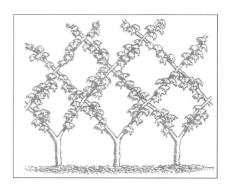

Belgian fence pattern results from the crossing of branches from several double cordon plants.

training espalier

If planning free-standing espalier, establish the framework with posts and wire stretched between them. You may have to attach wires to the wall also to secure the branches in the planned pattern. Position the selected plants at least 30cm from the wall or under the free-standing wires.

After planting, trim off all branches that do not lie in the same plane as the wall or wire. This will be all you need to start a natural or fan-shaped espalier. If planning to use a Y or U shaped pattern, trim off the leader and all but two side branches. For other patterns that need more height, let the leader reach the desired point before trimming it.

Using twine, secure stems to the wire or wall. Tie stems loosely so bark or leaves will not be damaged. As the plant grows, side branches can be removed as required to form intricate patterns.

Regularly remove any stems that grow out of the plane. You'll probably be able to rub off buds that are facing the wrong direction, rather than pruning. Make sure the plant you select can cope with the heat of the wall and will not be overcome with fungal problems resulting from reduced air circulation. Vines can be positioned in decorative espalier fashion, forming a very much quicker effect. Check books for further information about espalier techniques.

Plants that adapt well to espalier work:

apples

camellia, sasanqua varieties

cherries, fruiting or ornamental

citrus, small-leaf varieties like chinotto
   orange, calamondin, cumquat

cotoneaster

crabapple

figs, fruiting and ornamental

firethorn

ginkgo

guava

holly

maple, Japanese

mulberry, black or white Morus varieties

pear

Designer: Christine Elsbury, NSW, Australia

Right: Here sasanqua camellias have been espaliered in Belgian fence style, the leader removed and two side shoots trained as a double cordon up the wall. They are attached to wires, some still to be covered. When they reach the top they will be trimmed off there. They are bound with twine as each branch crosses another. They are also trained around the creeping fig-filled arch. The other wall is covered with star jasmine in full flower.

Photo: Melinda Bargwanna Designer: Rob Henderson, NSW, Australia

Left: A slab of wall 2m high on a rooftop garden has been dressed with a sasanqua camellia. Espalier can be shaped but casual as here, or neatly trimmed as desired, but pruning before stems get too woody will prevent scars being obvious on main branches.

81

The edible garden

USEFUL? MOST DEFINITELY. DECORATIVE? WHY NOT. POSSIBLE? OF COURSE. With the right choice of varieties, you will certainly be able to gather crops from your decorative potscaping to add that something special to your table. Harvestable plants can blend very attractively and not look out of place beside any plants. Tuck some mignonette lettuce in with the violas, place a pot of English spinach to leaf richly beside the azalea, or put a lemon tree, scenting the air when in blossom, then hung with golden fruit, alongside a bare magnolia and golden-leafed geranium. Or they can become the main event: vegetables and herbs in close combination, making a feature of the contrasts of their leaf shape, colour and texture, arranged as one arranges any group of pots. Paint a scene with red- and white-stemmed silverbeet or chard mixed in a big tub, alongside staked tomatoes reaching tall, or purple climbing beans growing up a tripod, leafy 'cut and come again' mesclun lettuces at their feet, a generous pot of parsley, and a smaller one of chives. A trough of varietal lettuces can be set on a windowsill, hanging baskets can grow herbs or strawberries, and trellises can allow your crops to climb upward should extra space be required.

Care is needed when selecting pots. Make sure they are large enough for the roots of vigorously growing vegetables. However, you may have to move them around to catch the sun, and for harvesting and repotting. Plastic pots are ideal as they are light and moisture will not evaporate from their surfaces, but do make sure they will not become unstable with top-heavy growth. Terracotta, moulded concrete and cast stone pots offer stability, attractive colours and a vast range of shapes. Mobile pot stands are very useful with large pots. Place crocks or gravel at the base for drainage and some charcoal over this to act as a filter before filling up with best-quality potting mix laced with generous quantities of slow-release fertiliser, well composted manure or mushroom or garden compost. They will all help to provide the soil with excellent physical structure, plus nutrients and organisms to boost vegetable growth.

Right: Using a hanging basket provides more growing area, an opportunity to position them in more sunlight and an attractive ball of edible greenery. This one contains lettuce, parsley, chives and rocket, all of which can be harvested a few leaves at a time to make a salad or dress a plate. The petals of the French marigolds make a good splash of colour and can also be added for a piquant bite in salads. Replace the lettuce as it starts to flower, as leaves become bitter.

Seanna McCune's garden, NSW, Australia

Left: Leafy vegetables like spinach, lettuce, cabbage, parsley and chives need nitrogen-rich liquid manure showers every two weeks, wetting the leaves and the potting mix. Apply after the sun has left them for the day so they won't burn. Flowering vegetables like beans, cucumbers, tomatoes and broccoli need nitrogen during the first month to get them well-established, but general fertiliser containing phosphorus and potassium to follow, thus encouraging flower and later, fruit development. Root crops like beetroot, radish or carrots need the same treatment. Fish or seaweed fertilisers will provide all these organically if preferred. Here a bowl of buttercrunch lettuce has been raised in maximum sunlight with a large pot of shop-bought green onions growing as they wait to be harvested, a few at a time. Chilli seedlings await planting out in pots, with a pink miniature rose adding colour and contrast.

When selecting vegetables, choose mini or compact varieties that have been specially developed for pot growth, and early maturing varieties that will speed up production rates. Another way to speed up production is to buy small established plants — it's faster than growing from seed. But take care the plants are still in active new growth and haven't developed a thickened stem. This can indicate that they are near the end of their life cycle and are exhausted

from life in a very confined pot. If space is limited it is wise to plant vegetables that can be continually harvested, like leaves of soft-hearting lettuces, senposai, silverbeet or rocket, rather than types that reach maturity slowly and then are removed completely. Gather beans, peas, cucumbers and tomatoes regularly to keep them producing. When young fruit is harvested, the plant must continue to develop more, as its purpose in life is to produce

seed. Pull up root vegetables when they are small and compact and haven't become woody. Test their size by running your fingers around the root top at the base of the stems. Compact carrots are best eaten once the top is 2 to 4cm across, baby beets and Japanese turnips at golf ball size. Select varieties suitable for the season and your climate, although if you have a microclimate in certain parts of your garden, that will extend the growing season.

Above: Ornamental kale glows richly pink or purple all through winter. It is usually grown for its ornamental value, but occasional leaves can be harvested and used as contrast in cabbage salads and mixed lettuce salads. Frilly green-leafed mustard kale makes an interesting potted plant and is a sharp-tasting addition to salads.

Above: This trough has been planted with three lettuce varieties: mizuna, radicchio and oak-leaf. All can combine or be used individually by taking a few leaves at a time from the outside of each plant. It won't feed a hungry family but will make a salad for one or two every week and a few leaves will provide variety to a traditional green salad. Feed the plants every two weeks with liquid fertiliser and keep them well watered. When they start to flower, remove them, turn the soil over and add a generous supply of slow-release fertiliser with the extra potting mix to top it up. Plant dwarf peas, beans or root vegetables next to efficiently use the nutrients in the potting mix.

leafy vegetables for pots

broccoli, mini varieties are most suitable. Cool weather crops, full sun and must be well fed.

cabbage, compact growers most suitable. Feed and water well, cool climate growers.

cauliflower, mini varieties best, full sun, winter growers.

combo lettuce varieties, mixed red and green leaf open-hearted lettuces, use outer leaves as they grow.

endive, curly bitter green salad mixer, grows best in cooler months.

kale, mustard, curly-leafed and hot tasting; ornamental, decorative purple and pink leaves, can be eaten.

lambs lettuce, also called corn salad, soft green leaves for salads. Grows spring into summer, semi-shade.

mesclun mixes, mixed leaf lettuce varieties, use outer leaves as they grow, mild winter and summer growers.

mignonette lettuces, open-hearted lettuce varieties red or green available. Grow to full size or use as they grow, full sun and regular fertiliser.

mizuna, feathery leaves, mild taste. 'Cut-and-come-again', summer and mild winter grower, full sun.

pak choi, usually harvested whole but can be used a couple of leaves at a time, full sun, feed well.

radicchio, winter growing into red, strong-flavoured hearting clump, can use leaves a few at a time.

rocket, grows through both winter and summer in mild climates, plant replacements as it comes to flower each season, full sun.

senposai, neat leafy oriental vegetable, harvest a few leaves at a time for stirfries, full sun, feed well.

silverbeet, white-, red- and yellow-stemmed and compact varieties available, feed well, full sun.

spinach, English, plant successive groups in cool months in full sun, feed well, harvest whole plant.

Left: Solidly alone in a heavy pot stands a well-staked capsicum, this one ripened to red. One of the pleasures of potted vegetables is the fact that you can turn them to the sun or shade as required, this having chased the sun to ripen it fast. More flowers up the stem promise future crops this summer. Prune the plant back in autumn, apply topping-up manure and set aside till next spring. Chillies also make a useful pot plant and many varieties are available. They are treated in the same way as capsicums and look decorative. Be sure to warn young children that they must not play with them.

fruiting varieties

beans, bush and climbing, yellow butter beans and purple varieties make nice contrasts. Grow on trellis or tepee shapes in summer, full sun, harvest regularly.

capsicum, attractive sub-shrub, full sun, water and feed regularly, fruits develop slowly.

chilli, all varieties, summer producing sub-shrubs. Useful and ornamental, full sun.

cucumber, space-saver compacts or trained up a trellis, plant seedlings in spring.

mini melons, plant in spring, full sun, feed well.

peas, dwarf varieties suit hanging basket or pot with trellis for support.

pumpkins, mini varieties, as for melons.

snow peas, as for peas.

tomatoes, particularly mini varieties, colour and shape variations available.

Above: Looking very sparsely planted in a 35cm bowl is a Thai chilli, a mini orange tomato, Welsh onions and a couple of seeds of compact cucumber. The healthiest seedling will be retained. In six weeks the tomato is fruiting, onions clumping and at the back the cucumber is trailing and the chilli flowering and thickening up. Welsh onions can be used as chives or pulled up as green onions. The Thai chilli carries green, red and purple fruit. This mini vegetable patch was still producing three months later.

fruit

apple, buy plants grafted onto dwarfing root stocks, dwarf cultivars available.

citrus, cumquat, calamondin, lemon, particularly Lisbon, lime, Kaffir lime. Use large pots, top up potting mix and slow-release fertiliser regularly, don't let them become too dry.

fig, use a heavy pot, full sun. Copes with dry conditions.

guava, all varieties evergreen and attractive, keep well watered.

olive, drought- and wind-tolerant, large pot, full sun.

peach, dwarf varieties most suitable, full sun, buy variety to suit your area.

pear, dwarf varieties, cool conditions.

pineapple, plant top 2cm slice with leafy top, full sun, warm conditions.

strawberry, buy new virus-free varieties or small, non-running alpine type. Use large tub, hanging basket or traditional strawberry pot, full sun, well watered and fed.

pomegranate, select a fruiting, not ornamental variety, deciduous, spines on stem ends, full sun.

Above: This lemon trimmed with golden fruit is a Lisbon, the best variety for pot growth. They crop heavily in winter but will produce occasional fruit throughout the year. As a compact specimen in a pot it is easier to deal with aphids, stink bugs, scale and leaf miner, which are frequent but easily controlled problems with citrus. Lime, kaffir lime and cumquats make excellent pot plants. Keep them pruned and well watered.

Below: Excellent examples of root vegetables that do well in pots: radish, turnip, carrots and green onions. Radish and green onions need less depth then carrots, beets and turnips. Rotate root crops with beans, peas and later leafy vegetables.

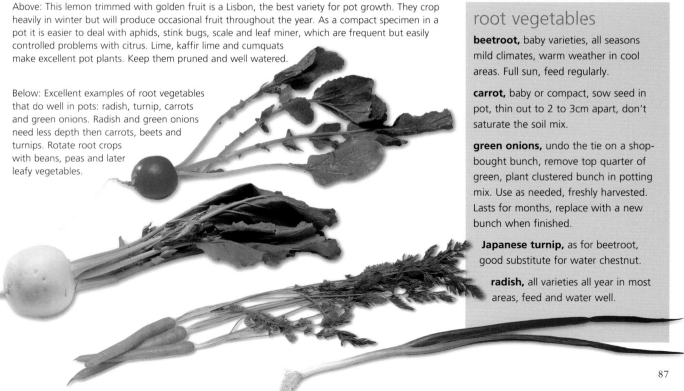

root vegetables

beetroot, baby varieties, all seasons mild climates, warm weather in cool areas. Full sun, feed regularly.

carrot, baby or compact, sow seed in pot, thin out to 2 to 3cm apart, don't saturate the soil mix.

green onions, undo the tie on a shop-bought bunch, remove top quarter of green, plant clustered bunch in potting mix. Use as needed, freshly harvested. Lasts for months, replace with a new bunch when finished.

Japanese turnip, as for beetroot, good substitute for water chestnut.

radish, all varieties all year in most areas, feed and water well.

Below: To make herbs part of a display you need healthy plants and a few props. This curly-leafed parsley growing in a low pot looks delightfully rounded. A sphere of sandstone repeats the form and the duck lightens the scene. To harvest the parsley, take stems from the base and the outside of the plant, not the centre. Continually turn the pot so each side is used and its sun exposure is even. Flat-leafed or continental parsley and chervil are alternatives. They are all biennials, growing vigorously for the first year and a half, but losing leaf vigour as they start to flower. Start a new pot early to continue supplies.

Above: Don't over-plant when preparing a mini-herb garden. These three herbs, chives, bush basil and lemon thyme, bought in 10cm pots, are enough for a 20 to 25cm pot. In six weeks time they have robustly filled it and are used frequently. The small growing bush basil is an excellent choice for pots. It's compact, generously leafy and as well-flavoured as sweet basil.

Above: Herbs filling a lined wire basket, positioned near the kitchen and in good sun, can be both convenient for culinary use and attractive. Mint and oregano are especially good in pots or baskets because they are invasive in the garden. This collection prettily masses coloured and variegated leaves to lift the predominantly lush green growth. Sprouting generously at the top are chives and curly-leafed parsley, with golden oregano and marjoram surrounding them. A gently sprouting bush basil is developing among them, a good choice here as its small leaves do not prevent sun getting to the other herbs. Below hang variegated mint and summer savory. Water and feed these plants regularly but always wash the leaves before use to remove any fertiliser residue. Turn the basket as you harvest, taking a few leaves from several plants to keep it looking leafy. Nip the growing tips of oregano, marjoram, mint and basil regularly for the kitchen, thus keeping the plants compact. Cut individual chives from the base so regrowth will be strong.

herbs

basil, sweet in large pot, bush basil more compact. Feed and water well, grows in summer, full sun.

bay, topiaried or free-growing evergreen, move to larger pots as it grows, full to part sun.

chervil, fine-leafed parsley type, will grow two years, semi-shade in summer, full sun in winter.

chives, will die down in winter, re-emerge for summer. Resents crowding, full sun. Garlic chives have good flavour.

coriander, full sun, tends to bolt. Try Vietnamese mint as substitute.

dill, needs a deep pot and staking or other plants to support it. Fine and feathery, lasts 2 or 3 months, full sun.

lemon grass, dense grassy clump for large pot, full sun and moisture. Cut back after winter for regrowth.

marjoram, low, clumping perennial, good in mixed pots, trim off after winter, full sun.

mint, many varieties, needs lots of moisture and full sun or light shade.

mint, Vietnamese, strongly scented, leafy even through winter, full sun or part shade.

oregano, clumping perennial, golden- and green-leafed varieties, full sun.

parsley, lasts a year or two, replace once it's gone to seed, feed and water well, full or part sun.

rosemary, shrubby upright and cascading forms available, likes a dry sunny position.

sage, coloured leaf and standard grey-leaf forms, must be dry and sunny.

savory, summer annual and winter perennial types, low clumping and flowering, full sun.

tarragon, summer leafy stems, dies back in winter, needs a tall pot, full sun.

thyme, marvellous pot plants, many flavours and colourings, full sun, not over-watered.

watercress, likes a very damp pot, will trail from a basket, semi-shade.

Design inspiration

THE CONTINUING SUCCESS OF OPEN GARDEN SCHEMES, NATIONAL AND worldwide garden tours, television gardening programmes and a constantly burgeoning supply of ever-tempting gardening publications, indicates that gardeners love to look, to be inspired, to learn and to experience something a little different. You may be new to gardening, and designing your first deck or courtyard planting. You may be an old hand, recently moved to a different environment, or simply wanting a change. For all these and countless more reasons we are all out to find some inspiration, some ideas, some techniques or some themes that will set us on our way. The delightful thing is that the way each individual makes use of this inspiration will turn it into a distinctly individual design. So here's a look over some people's garden walls. The owners are pleased to let you see how they have handled their sites, dealt with their problems and decorated their space.

Above: A flower-filled deck in autumn is rich with pink, purples and white contrasts. Frosty carex is silvery, in front of a pink salvia, busy lizzies and budding chrysanthemum and a white-dotted polka dot plant. Blood grass and a bronze flax provide strappy shapes among full heads of sedum and hydrangea species. The cat enjoys the view.

Right: French-style architecture with a paved courtyard and pool has been softened with raggedly individual climbing iceberg roses and a prostrate rosemary hedge. In winter its blue flowers repeat the blue of the pool.

Designer: Christine Elsbury, NSW, Australia

making an entry

Four potplanted portals, all distinctly different.
Left: Neoclassic elegance with flagstone paving, cast stone pillars and balcony edging, paired pots of blue-grey-leafed *Kalanchoe pumila* and mop-topped cumquats, and a plinth against the house is graced with a pair of *Dracaena draco* perfectly suited to their pots. Neatly trimmed box fills the troughs. This planting suits subtropical, Mediterranean and frost-free temperate climates.

Designer: Peter Fudge, NSW, Australia

Below: Vireyas are part of the rhododendron family, but they thrive in hot humid conditions as opposed to the frost-hardy 'rhodos'. They need a rich acid soil and good drainage and must be frequently watered. They flower through spring in generous heads.

Designer: Peter Fudge, NSW, Australia

Above: This front door is dressed with a pair of vireyas, looking a touch theatrical but appealing, in bloom at present, deliciously green and lush the rest of the year. They are happy in dappled sunlight.

Below: Several treeferns, *Cyathea australis*, *macrozamia*, *monsteria*, *Philadendron selloum*, and an assortment of palms surround the trunk of a cotton palm. A small water garden, another traditional Balinese garden feature, holds a planting of several marginal water plants — pickerel rush, arum, cyperus and a water iris. The large basket holding their roots has been rested on bricks to bring them to just below the water surface and positioned at one side so fish and water are visible. A golden Balinese flag on a bamboo pole flutters whenever there's a breeze.

Designer: Bali in Profile, NSW, Australia

Above: A handsomely carved front gate opens into a tiny courtyard and doorway delightfully decorated in Balinese style. The carved door surround is from a temple and is attached to the architrave. Both it and the gates were brought from Bali as were the carved statues of flower-decked gods that offer welcome at the entry. Traditionally in Bali, flowers are replaced daily.

Designer: Bali in Profile, NSW, Australia

Designer: Peter Fudge, NSW, Australia

Left: A prettily patterned door in a paved entrance court is flanked by two neatly clipped topiary box spheres, in very restrained but appropriate style. One plant has alyssum at its feet. It will cascade in the same manner as the babies' tears have in the other pot. Other alternatives for groundcover plants include verbena, lobelia, thyme, or sweet violets providing flower colour; and ivy, mondo grass, ajuga, sedums or ground ivy for a green-only scene. Whatever is planted, it is important that the stem of the standard is not obscured and at least some of the rich pot colour is visible.

Photo: Gil Hanly Barbara Garret's garden, N. Z.

courtyards and decks

Above: The surface treatment chosen depends on how much walking you want to do. If the courtyard is a main thoroughfare or outdoor living area, the surface must be level and durable. This courtyard uses concrete in a brushed aggregate finish, with tiles neatly edging the gardens and patterning the wide expanses. It is also patterned by the covered drains which carry away rain and hosing floods. The surface is excellently slip-free. Shaped beds divide the area into pathway and garden room sections, and are wide enough for different plantings each side of a vine-covered lattice.

The predominant use of white flowers in the climbing rose, the flowering pyracantha entwined on the lattice, the shrub roses and the nicotiana in the beds, along with the clipped box hedging, makes each room different, but linked. A pair of mop-head robinias stand in pots with mini mondo edging, and a pink rose climbs over the pink-toned brickwork at the gate. This is an attractive way to divide a large area, providing privacy, enclosure and a neat but pretty garden scene. It could easily convert to a range of plants to specifically suit your climate, colour choice or favourites.

Wood is frequently used on decks and verandahs and imparts its own patina and mood. It is wise to select the best quality hardwood your budget will allow when constructing new decking, and maintain it with regular coats of staining paint or oils to reduce wood rot, slime and moulds. Prevent the build-up of slimy areas with applications of bleach or mould-removers. Regularly check the base of pots and furniture out in the weather on wood, as constant damp causes wood to rot. Pots are best on feet or stands so there is air between the surfaces, but even then move them and furniture regularly.

Below: This deck was constructed to raise the level of the garden below, lifting it to reach more sun and to become part of the higher garden. A delightfully eclectic collection of plants and pots provide colour and patterning, and the eye can wander to points of interest at every angle. The blue-grey-leafed succulent is the clustering moonstones, *Pachyphytum oviferum*, alone on one side and planted with grasses, a scirpus and lomandra, providing a spiky contrast on the other. Two miniature roses, 'The Fairy', pink,

and 'Green Ice', white-tinged green, will flower most of spring, summer and into autumn and make ideal pot plants. A green pine stands tall in contrast to the blue-grey dwarf, *Abies concolor* 'Compacta', in a small upright pot on the table. Splashes of colour are provided by red dwarf salvia, orange French marigolds and a cluster of white chalet daisies. This is a plant collector's not an entertainer's deck, so it provides the merest nod to seated comfort, but plants are portable and arrangable should the need for more open area arise.

Photo: Gil Hanly Armstrong garden, NZ

Left: Brick paving provides a durable, smooth surface, clean clear access, an easy technique to build in level changes and pocket gardens as well as colour and patterning possibilities. It also produces a casual, cottagey feel to the landscaping. House bricks however, are more porous than many of the purpose-made pavers and can become mossy in rainy spells or in damp areas. The moss and slipperiness can be removed by brushing on household bleach, pool chlorine or copper sulphate solution. Here, the pink of the pathway is repeated in the variegated star jasmine leaves, *Trachelospermum jasminoides* ' Tricolor', and the flower stems of the silvery leafed *Plectranthus argentatus*. Budding heads of valerian, *Centranthus ruber*, give promise of more red-pink tones, supported by rich purple leaves of sun-strengthened ajuga. Hydrangea and a shrubby buddleja cluster around the bird bath.

Designer: Michael Cooke, NSW, Australia

Left: The paving here is not the main event, but just enough is spared to allow feet through the pretty mass of potted and paving-grown flowering treasures. A fig offers the first of the season's fruits to the sun. At its feet is a sparkling red *Helianthemum* 'Fire Dragon'. Behind this are the fluffy seedheads of an alpine anemone, *Pulsatilla alpina*. A large gloxinia is leafing up in the shade, and ambling about in the corner is *Campanula poscharskyana* with blue-mauve flowers. The white flowers on silvery foliage are shrubby *Convolvulus cneorum*. Standing tall behind is Jerusalem sage, seen also in front with its whorls of flowers circling up the stems. The other grey leafy spires are flower heads of lambs ears, *Stachys byzantina*. Small leaves and flowers feature on the *Hydrangea scandens*. Below it is a pot of *Brachyscome* 'Break o' Day' with its pink-mauve daisies. In the terracotta pot is *Euphorbia myrsinites*. The walls are draped in a twining yellow-leafed hop.

Right: The large concrete pavers used in this courtyard provide a spacious feel, and are detailed by the planting patterns in spaces left unfilled. The central space of four tiles gives enough room for a silver birch to grow and spread, providing winter sun and summer shade, as well as a focal point to the paving. The pavers are laid on sand, essential to supply air and water to the tree's roots. This tree does not like dry soil so keep it well watered. Ants, the reason for the tiny hillocks of sand between the pavers, can be discouraged by filling the holes with common salt. Salt is also an excellent killer of weeds in paving cracks. Ajuga has been used as a living mulch under the birch and repeated as the infill in the stepping stones. Box hedging borders the pavers. Beyond is a flagstone area at a slightly higher level with Virginia creeper trailed along to conceal the edging. A neat row of symmetrical pots planted with viola have been lined up cleverly to delineate the step.

Designer: Harris Hobbs Landscapes, Canberra, NSW

97

Above: A beautifully bright potted collection clusters around two white flowering bougainvilleas, which have been well clipped back after each flowering. Red comes from the salvias, coleus leaves, begonias and poinsettia. Yellows are provided by a kalanchoe, coreopsis and pelargonium leaves. Pinks and whites appear among the busy lizzies and twining mandevillea buds and blooms. Pots of liriope and a pteris fern supply green and white streaky foliage.

Below: This symphony in grey and mauve with notes of pink and yellow has been composed from the ground up. A circular pond with its radiating spokes in-filled with grey gravel sets the scene, a part of a design rather than a heavy duty surface. Two catmint varieties flowering mauve here are *Nepeta* x *faassenii*, low near the seat, and a couple of *N.* 'Six Hills Giant' standing high. Flower spires emerging above the clumps of grey lambs ears will open in more mauve. Lavenders, allards *L.* x *allardii*, with tall buds near the seat, and French, *L. dentata*, a lower clump, provide more grey leafy bulk and more mauve-blue flowers. The round leaf blue-grey cluster is *Thalictrum aquilegiifolium*, its tall spires opening mauve in summer. Flowers of deep red and white on grey stems are rose campion, *Lychnis coronaria*, a biennial that seeds itself generously, comes in these two colours only, and grows from a flat grey-leafed plant. Reaching tall well behind the seat is a Scotch thistle, *Onopordum acanthum*, wonderfully silver but very spiky. As an annual it is replaced each year. More background grey shrubs include the twiggy germander, *Teucrium fruticans*, and the large segmented leaves of honey flower, *Melianthus major*. The honey flower spikes are just coming up to open, with yellow-cream heads. More yellow comes from the tiny buttons of green-leafed lavender cotton, *Santolina rosmarinifolia*, the choice of the green form making a wise contrast here. There comes a time when more is too much. A generous spurge, *Euphorbia characias*, is included for its grey foliage and limey flowers in summer. Leaves of another thistle safely unfurl behind it. Towering at the back are foxgloves indicating this is a cool climate garden, but the majority of the plants used here happily grow in Mediterranean and subtropical zones.

Photo: Gil Hanly Elspeth Shannon's garden, NZ

styled to suit

It's your courtyard, it should suit you. Consider how much time you want to spend there, both to maintain it and to relax in it. What are its main purposes? Children's play area, drying space, dining and entertaining areas or simply a space for absolute solitude? How much do you want to spend on it and how quickly do you want it 'finished'? They will all have an impact on the ultimate choices. Your own personal style will create something individually yours, no matter where you got your inspiration. Here are some more dream scenes.

Above: Screen fixtures such as clothes lines with brush fencing. The sun and breezes can reach the washing, but it doesn't dominate the area. Another technique is to fit retractable or moveable lines. Keep them well maintained so they won't seize.

Photo: Gil Hanly Robin Rive's garden, NZ

Above: Storage and garbage areas can be screened with brush fencing, a hedge or a vine-wrapped wooden fence. It's simple, attractive and effective. Star jasmine has been used here.

Above: Japanese garden design involves transforming tiny spaces into vignettes of nature where less is probably more than enough. A few well chosen rocks are wrapped but not obscured with moss and several ferns, and a pine is positioned bonsai-like on the largest. Another, with its feet among rocks, collects magnolia petals falling from the neighbour's tree. A very happy juxtaposition. It would be advisable to control the growth of the pines with bonsai techniques by keeping them in large pots submerged under the moss, otherwise they'll grow out of proportion to the site. Dwarf varieties could also suit. Rushes, just recovering from a pruning tidy, will bulk out and form a contrasting shape to the ferns. A stone lantern is functional and decorative.

Below: This hilly site has been stepped and levelled to produce a flowery bower, good to look down into and delightful to sit in. The bricks at the base were laid in concentric circles, patterned by using differing facets and centred with an infill of basket-weave design. Brick walled beds support the level changes, and are draped with flowers or support pots. Pink and white have been studiously selected with an occasional nod to plum and grey foliage. The flowering cherry will be followed in summer with pink puffs on the silk tree, *Albizia julibrissen*. Foxgloves stand resplendent above lupins, roses, dahlias and nicotiana. A sea of foaming white iberis, salvia and Venus's navelwort, *Omphalodes linifolia*, link and soften the display.

Photo: Gil Hanly Dr Bryan and Jan Oldham's garden, NZ

Left: Water is an essential in Japanese-styled gardens, both for the sight of a reflective surface, as in ceremonial stone bowls, or for the sounds of it moving, as in shishi-o-doshi or this nagatoi water spout. The dampened area is filled with assorted pebbles, and marginal water plants form leafy contrasts. Dwarf papyrus, mondo grass clumps and scirpus with strelitzia in the corner complete the water garden feel.

Below: Steps and walled gardens cope with height changes, formality and informality nicely blended with a pot of golden carex. Lush mondo grass dresses the steps, a spring-leafed Virginia creeper ambles up a pillar, topped with a miniature crepe myrtle. Well trimmed box and a standard ball of conifer present orderliness. Bright faces of viola team with white primula in a giant pot that is also home to a climbing white iceberg rose. There are spillovers of seaside daisy and violas at the edges.

Photo: Gil Hanly Sally Mason's garden, NZ

Above: Here the central pool is wrapped in green with a clipped box border and the paving is circled with raised beds of mossy bricks planted with draping shrubs and perennials. White is the predominant contrast colour used. The effect is cool and calm. On both sides of the gateway pillars, (restrainedly topped with empty urns) are *Iris confusa*, which enjoy rocky sites in semi-shade. Seaside daisy, a fuchsia and white-flowered honesty lead round to white-decked *Viburnum plicatum*. A climbing white rose and another viburnum stand under a still leafless ginkgo. Autumn colour from them all will be splendid. The sweeping green stems on the other side of the pillar are scented Solomon's seal, a perennial that dies down each winter. Shade, coolness and adequate water keep this courtyard green and lush. A similar style could easily be planted with tropical and subtropical varieties.

Left: Here is a typical Mediterranean courtyard with flagged flooring and many doorways leading to dark coolness inside. A deciduous vine covers a stoutly supported pergola. It provides summer shade at the table. The winter sun has warmed the flags and house walls and will be diminished as leaves develop. Actually, here it is flowers that develop first on this wisteria, and after about a month of perfumed petalled grape-like bunches, the divided leaves will cover the stems. A large tub of geranium was the winter feature and will be moved to a sunnier spot as the shade extends. A tub of begonias, hydrangea, bay or ferns could replace it for summer. Between each door grow Mexican orange blossom, *Choisya ternata*, with perfumed flowers in spring and sometimes autumn and aromatic foliage to brush past all year. The table and chairs invite you to linger.

Left: Two settings offered in this herb-filled courtyard, one under the grapevine against the house with cafe style chairs and table, the other under a market umbrella in generous cane chairs in a bank of varietal thymes. Bay, clipped box and basil are richly dark green against the white wall with a tall stand of salvia about to provide red flower highlights. A potted tree of camellia guards the door and a young lemon verbena and pot-controlled mint sit by the dry stone wall. Grey foliage of celmesia displays the upright daisy heads. As a foil to them is a purple-leafed Judas tree. The rest of the bank is planted with cascades of flowering thyme and trim cushions of leafy thyme using such varieties as 'Anderson's Gold', 'Westmoreland', 'Purpureus', 'Silver Posy', 'Elfin', woolly, caraway and lemon-scented. Plant several of the same variety rather than a string of different ones so there will be some link in the design. They are generally hardy but don't really thrive in humid conditions.

garden seating

Seating can be placed in a shady cool spot, protected from summer sun, or in winter, in a sun-warmed site to heat up chilled bones. A garden seat can be a place to rest and draw breath, it can be a place from which to observe the garden or a view, and it will always be the place on which things are put. It can also be a decorative device, creating a focal point at the end of a pathway, or a patch of colour or a shape that contrasts with the surroundings.

Right: This lush tropical-looking hideaway is screened by tall golden champaca, *Michelia champaca*, an evergreen tree with scented creamy flowers from mid-summer into autumn. A giant elephant's ear, *Alocasia macrorrhiza*, stands lushly green in the centre. The large attractive leaves of a native hydrangea, *Abrophyllum ornans*, are crowned with wide clusters of creamy-green perfumed flowers in spring with infill of palms and ivy groundcover.

Designer: Peter Nixon, NSW, Australia

Left: Chairs and a table can provide the spot for a tea or coffee break, the setting for a long leisurely lunch or the set for a candle-lit dinner. Restrained simplicity in the design and decor of a tiled verandah, with a grape trellis over the unpainted table and benches plays off well against the strong mustard of the walls and rich mauve of the woodwork. The supporting potted colour of the same mauve felicia on its own, petunias in a hanging basket and diascia growing with mustard bright nasturtiums simply strengthen the statement. Tumbling seaside daisy, geraniums and viola dress the brick steps.

Photo: Gil Hanly Jane Evans' garden, NZ

Right: The corner of this enclosed courtyard is effectively screened with a lattice-backed, arched seat of treated pine set into the ground among a veritable forest of palms. Shade and seclusion are assured. The densely clumping bamboo palm with elegant stems is *Chamaedorea costaricana*, its drooping leaves producing a wide crown. A kentia, *Howea forsteriana*, supports the act. In front, in semi-shade are pots of shiny-leafed *Fatsia japonica*, palmlike *Cycas revoluta*, a pair of topiaried lilypillies, *Syzygium* 'Bush Christmas', and golden *Carex oshimensis* 'Evergold'. Planted underneath the seat is mondo grass, supported in a pot alongside with the black-leafed form in the centre and the mini form around it.

Pictured at Rast Bros. Nursery, NSW, Australia

Designer: Peter Fudge, NSW, Australia

roof gardens

Above: Clay pavers are used here with detailed patterning in the first section of a rooftop garden. The lavender garden beyond is more casually paved with a line of stepping stones. Under any rooftop paving or garden, waterproofing is the first requirement, followed by the search for vital information concerning how much weight of soil, water and paving the slab or roof has been designed to hold. Check with architects or engineers before starting work. Gardens are a constantly moist environment and water will find its way through any cracks or weaknesses. Waterproof membrane, laid under paving, pots or beds is

essential. It must not be pierced, and paving is positioned on it. Where gardens are planned, agricultural pipes are layed and directed to an outlet that can handle the flow. A layer of aggregate covers the piping and the membrane before potting mix is added. There are some light mixes of potting material that will help reduce the weight, but always factor in the extra weight of wet soil and foliage. Waterproofing and draining experts will provide the service or give the right advice. In this garden neat screens of clipped *Murraya paniculata* back the garden. Planted in front at 3m intervals are Chinese tallows, *Sapium sebiferum*, looking stark and structural now with orange trunks, becoming leafy in spring and summer and resplendent with fiery colour

in autumn. Grey-leafed germander, *Teucrium fruticans*, can be neatened to fit between the gardenias planted in front, or both left to grow into each other. White busy lizzie provides winter colour, and mondo grass softens the edge. Tiny cushions of violet divide the high edge and the stepping stones. A large square of French lavender, *Lavandula dentata*, provides a sea of grey foliage with blue flower heads predominantly through winter but spasmodically the rest of the year. Keep cutting off spent flowers. More clipped shaping of a box hedge surrounds tapering chamaecyparis. The large spreading jacaranda beyond grows outside the garden but its beautiful spring colour has influenced the choices made here.

Below: The piping Pan has been positioned in front of a mirror to increase the light source and extend the image of the area of water. Water is pumped through his pipe and trickles back into the pool below, softly musical and relaxing. A large planter on both sides contains a compact Bull Bay magnolia cultivar, a creeping fig to wander either side up the wall, stephanotis that flowers all summer as a frame around the mirror, and box borders.

Above: Two scenes on this sun-facing rooftop garden that has been designed as viewspace, living space and an attractively landscaped scene to live with. In cool weather the sun/rain screen is rolled back to bathe the deck and interior tiles in sun for warmth. In hot summer sun and during rain spells, the outdoor living area is still usable with the acrylic screen extended to cover doorways and the dining area, an area of 5 square metres. The fabric allows light in but cuts UV rays. Plantscaping includes four large clipped lilypillies and the fountain and planter box features described at right. Seasonal plantings are displayed on the dining table.

Designer: Annie Wilkes

Right: All of this roof planting is planted in purpose-built coloured fibreglass containers — cylinders for free-standing placement and rectangular boxes for positions against the wall. To keep the soil at a more stable temperature, the fibreglass is lined with polystyrene. The pots were filled with best quality potting mix and a drip watering system was fitted, as this is a windy, sunbaked site. Drainage pipes run from the interior of the boxes out to join roof drainage systems. This pretty planting contains a hardy variegated spider plant, generously flowered and leafed blue statice, *Limonium perezii*, a winter-flowering crassula, a fine-leafed atriplex, *Acacia sophorae*, and a *Eucalyptus luehmanniana*. Wind and their natural shape keep the height low to reveal the view.

Below: These well-leafed specimens grow in three large pots 1 metre high and 50cm in diameter and leaf up a large concrete expanse. They include varieties of banksia, teatree, eucalyptus, grevillea and lilypilly, growing strongly on a regime of Australian native plant food every 6 months and a drip watering sytem. The potting mix is topped up each 6 months also. Gravel at the base of each planter ensures good drainage. They will outgrow their containers and have to be replaced every 5 to 8 years.

Right: Agapanthus fill a central pot, leafy all year and decked with blue or white flower spikes through spring into summer. Planted behind are one of the Virginia creepers that leaf up the walls through the warm months and colour well in autumn. This deck is part of a common room that is open to all residents.

All pictured at 'Sirius', Department of Housing, NSW, Australia

Above: A coppery-leafed she-oak, *Allocasuarina torulosa*, frames the view and the border planting of lower shrubs like atriplex varieties, and others mentioned in the description opposite. There's also a tumbling mound of grey-leafed *Calocephalus brownii* with lavender, rosemary and other herbs nearest the doorway, beyond the colour-toned ventilation pipes. The tracery of Virginia creeper covers the concrete walls. The whole design creates secluded seating as well as access to a great view.

Problem solver

WILL THERE BE PROBLEMS? OF COURSE THERE WILL. PLANTS DO FAIL.
It happens in any garden, so it's not surprising for plants to fail in the artificial environment that a balcony, courtyard or pot creates. When a plant dies and you want to prevent another failure, tip the plant out of the pot and check the potting mix, the roots and the drainage.

failure of a plant

Dry crumbling mix indicates drought conditions, wet mix with rotting roots indicates poor drainage, a root-filled pot says potting-on was necessary, and fungal growths around roots or few roots remaining indicate disease. Check the basics of containment gardening on pages 4 to 17, detailing potting mix, containers, fertiliser and watering regimes and drainage. If these all appear to be in order, the problem could be too much or too little light. Plants will look pale, withered, yellow or brown-streaked, or crisped at the edges when in too much light. If they are leggy, leaning and poorly-leafed they will have struggled to reach more. Some of these signs also indicate fertiliser abuse. Similar indications are seen on plants suffering wind exposure, so check this as a possibility too.

Right: This richly foliaged and flowered set of pots shows how effective agapanthus can be in pots. The leaves are vigorous and lush all year as long as the pots receive slow-release fertiliser in early spring and at the end of summer. Trim off decaying leaves and watch for snails resting in the cool dark recesses. They will nibble leaves and flower buds if allowed. Keep the soil reasonably moist as pointed buds start to sprout and as flowers open. Even the seed heads look attractive at the end of summer but cut them back once they start to become ragged.

Another reason could be insect or disease attack. Insects are usually visible, even if wonderfully disguised. A good indicator is their piles of droppings around a pot, or chewed leaves. Caterpillars in their many varieties, will chew away at leaves and shred them, demolish them completely or skeletonise them. With potted plants it's best to pick them off or squash them with your hands, gloved if you prefer, rather than spray with chemicals in a confined space. Squashing allows you to release some vengeance as well.

There are many small insects with sucking mouthparts like aphids, thrips and mites that lie in leaf tips, mass up stems, under leaves and in buds. Evidence of their damage is mottling, wrinkling or wilting of leaves and malformed flowers. The leaves will eventually drop off and the plant can become denuded or unsightly. Scale insects, also suckers, attach themselves to stems and leaves, covering themselves with a protective shield-like shell. They cause streaking and eventual death of the leaf and will release sticky, shiny honeydew. This, and the black sooty mould that grows on it, is often the first indicator of scale problems. Ants often scurry about to gather the honeydew. Once again, in a small area it is best to use fingers to wipe or rub all these sucking insects off.

When watering, spray the undersides of leaves to discourage those insects like mites that like dry conditions. Methylated spirits on a cottonwool ball or stick can also be used to touch and kill each insect but it is too burning to wipe over leaf surfaces. There are proprietary brands of insecticides available but they can be toxic to humans when used in confined areas and can destroy beneficial insects.

Above: Dwarf sweet peas teamed with violas in a pot will make a pretty scene for winter in subtropical gardens, and spring in cooler areas. Violas are usually remarkably trouble-free but sweet peas can develop downy mildew which starts with yellowing of leaves, then a grey coating and death of the plant. It is worst in humid and rainy conditions.

Disease attacks are usually fungal and slowly spread. They can occur on stems, leaves, flowers or fruit. The affected area is often furry or soggy. It may be possible to remove the damaged leaves, alter the growing conditions by providing more light or air, and save the plant. With stem problems it's best to take cuttings well above the infected area, grow replacements and destroy the rest of the plant. For sooty mould, find the source of the honeydew, remove them and wash the plant clean. Rust on plants is coloured like its counterpart on metal but usually starts as small spots on upper and lower leaf surfaces. It can spread, link up, cause dead patches and can destroy the leaf and stem. Like moulds and mildews, it is associated with high humidity and poor air circulation, often occurring towards the end of the life cycle of the plant. Remove the leaves or plant, don't compost them, and let more air and sunlight into the area. There are fungicidal sprays available.

Another reason for plants to fail is just that it was the wrong plant for the site. Don't be discouraged. There are so many plants available, read up, question and experiment. Listed here are some sure-to-succeed varieties.

plants for full sun and wind exposure

tall growing varieties

Agonis flexuosa 'Nana' shiny willow-like leaves on rounded shrub.

Arbutus unedo, strawberry tree, sturdy deep-green evergreen, round leaves, white flowers and red berries, needs large pot and regular water.

Bambusa varieties, almost all of the bamboos produce dense foliage and cane screen.

Banksia varieties, most are suitable and dramatic.

Cacti, all varieties, can be combined with tree-like succulents.

Camellias, keep well clipped and well watered.

Citrus varieties, select small growers, water and feed well, keep well drained.

Conifers, select dwarf-growing varieties, water regularly.

Cordyline varieties, can grow tall or be maintained low, drooping grass-like foliage.

Dracaena varieties, dramatic shapes and colours, similar to cordylines.

Phormium tenax, New Zealand flax, dramatic upright leaves, various colours and dwarf forms available.

Ficus varieties, particularly fruiting fig and fiddle leaf fig.

Grevillea varieties, flower colour over long periods, must use fertiliser for Australian native plants.

Lauris nobilis, bay, deep green leaves, strong trunk can be topiaried.

Metrosideros varieties, New Zealand Christmas bush, various leaf colours on evergreen dense shrub, great windbreak.

Olea europaea, olive, grey leaves, allows light and view through.

Palms, most varieties, select a variety of heights, not just tall skinny ones, repot regularly.

Pittosporum tobira, densely bushy evergreen, perfumed white-cream flowers, berries follow.

Plumeria obtusa, frangipani, pipe-like stems topped with large boat-shaped leaves, perfumed flowers.

Left: Under the scented flowering arch of star jasmine are a pair of standardised durantas, a fast growing shrub that will need regular trimming to keep it in shape. Compare its growth to the one on the balcony on page 44. Below are pots of lavender, daisies and petunias, again needing regular trimming to keep them compact.

Designer: Peter Nixon, NSW, Australia

lower growers

Agapanthus varieties, broad strappy leaves with white, mauve or blue flower heads on strong stems.

Agave species, good shapes and colours.

Argyranthemum frutescens, Marguerite daisy, pink, white and yellow flowers, can be shaped, deadhead regularly.

Buxus varieties, free-growing or clipped.

Cactus varieties, extremely resistant to wind and sun.

Epidendrum ibaguense, Crucifix orchid, flowers almost all year.

Erigeron karvinskianus, seaside daisy, massed with pink and white flowers through warm months.

Euphorbia varieties, some succulents, some shrubby like spurge, poinsettia.

Felicia varieties, usually blue flowers, foliage various, deadhead regularly.

Helichrysum petiolare, small felty grey leaves.

Grasses, many varieties, colours and styles, great massed or added to mixed display.

Hebe varieties, various flower and leaf colours.

Herbs, particularly sage, thyme, rosemary and marjoram.

Lavandula species, both summer and winter bloomers, can stand alone or be included in mixed planting.

Pelargonium species, geranium, often grown for flower colour, many for foliage interest, very hardy.

Petunia varieties, annual, summer-flowering, must trim regularly for compact growth, good cut flower.

Succulents, some green-leafed others grey, reddish or cream, useful fillers.

Tagetes species, French marigolds, bright show of colour summer or winter.

Westringia fruticosa, coast rosemary, fine grey-green leaves, pale mauve flowers.

climbers

Hedera species, ivies, can climb, drape or fill a shape, various leaf shapes and colours.

Ficus pumila, climbing fig, clinging vine, small juvenile leaves can grow larger if not trimmed.

Pandorea varieties, shiny dark leaves, pink-, cream- or white-flowered varieties, a twiner.

Right: Camellias will grow well on exposed sites but will hold flowers longer and grow more lush in protected positions. The begonia in front needs screening from strong winds and semi-shade for leaves to be lush. Paired here they get morning sun only.

plants needing some wind and sun protection

tall growers

Acer palmatum, Japanese maple, good form, leaf colour and seasonal changes, needs moisture.

Acmena smithii, lilypilly, dense shrub, compact forms available.

Bambusa varieties, all the bamboos.

Begonia varieties with cane stems.

Camellia species, sasanquas flower in autumn, reticulatas and japonicas in winter or spring, lovely glossy leaves and many flower forms and colours, keep moist.

Citrus varieties, select more open forms like lemon or lime, need 6 hours' sun.

Malus varieties, apples, crabapple, keep well watered.

Musa species, bananas, dramatic foliage but need space.

Palms, most varieties can cope with some shade.

Prunus varieties, plums, cherries, peaches etc, keep well watered.

Salix species, willows, tortured and pussy willow well suited, keep well watered.

Schefflera arboricola , tall reaching canes covered with strong divided leaves.

Syzygium species, lilypilly, attractive pink new foliage, dense glossy leaves, compact forms available.

lower plants

Azalea varieties, various sizes and colours, some autumn- and winter-flowering.

Begonia varieties, some purely leafy, others grown for flowers.

Dahlia varieties, dwarf forms most suited.

Fuchsia varieties, must be protected from winds, good mixed or as stand-alone specimens.

Gardenia species, glossy leaves, white perfumed flowers in warm months, pick off all spent flowers.

Helichrysum petiolare 'Aureum', felty rounded lime-yellow leaves, long wandering stems.

Houttuynia cordata, green-leafed; 'Chameleon', variegated with pink-red highlights, dies down in winter.

Hydrangea varieties, mop-heads, lace caps and many other forms, keep moist and out of afternoon sun.

Nicotiana species, an annual with warm season flowers in a variety of colours.

Primula varieties, annual, winter and spring flowers, very reliable.

Succulents, some prefer semi-shade.

climbers

Akebia quinata, chocolate vine, evergreen in mild areas, soft leaves, brown-purple scented flowers in spring, keep watered.

Bougainvillea species, various foliage, form and flower colour, select and pot to suit.

Hoya varieties, twining climber with leathery leaves, waxy flowers in summer, likes to be pot-bound.

Lonicera species, honeysuckle, select less aggressive cultivars or giant Burmese variety, large pot.

Solanum varieties, white or blue flowers over long periods.

Trachelospermum jasminoides, star jasmine, evergreen with scented white flowers spring into summer.

Vitis vinifera, grape, ornamental and fruiting varieties, needs large pot.

Wisteria species, can be standardised or allowed to trail up a support; needs a large pot.

exposed sites

Wind can be the most devastating feature in a exposed site. In nature, plants grow low and are shaped to flow with it, then mound up to develop strength from their mass. This then creates more sheltered areas behind or below them. This should ideally be how one copes with an exposed roof garden or balcony, but usually there is insufficient space. A protective screen of well-watered shrubs and trees selected from the first list or from your observations of what copes well with this environment can be the barrier. The addition of a slatted or lattice screen secured to the walls will help break up the wind. Often a pane of glass can be fitted to actually divert its flow, however, divert is the word. The wind may well sweep back onto the site in another corner.

Protective layering of hardy leaves and stems is more effective, and less hardy species can be planted at their feet. Newly bought tall plants will always bare the brunt of the battering and will even suffer in eddies and back blasts. Select small species that can become acclimatised and grow up into the wind. Low pots of cacti and succulents or grasses arranged with weighty garden ornaments can be effective in difficult sites. Select heavy furniture or move lighter items inside the house and out again, as required, to prevent wind damage.

Below: Bamboo will make a good screen, even in exposed sites. Buy small plants, keep the pots well watered and fed, and allow them to grow into the space. Once established their canes break up the wind, make nice rustling and creaking noises and create a screen area for more delicate plants in front. Here an 'Autumn Joy' sedum, leafy carex and 'Blue Cape' plumbago cluster around a rustic seat.

Above: Clustering plants with comparable water requirements makes duties easier for carers. Here sedums and salvias with high drought tolerance are placed at the back, while several begonias, *Hydrangea aspera* and busy lizzies stand, easy to reach, at the front.

taking a holiday from your plants

Taking a holiday from a dependent contained garden can require almost as much preparation as for a dependent family; the more they are able to manage without constant ministrations the lighter will be your load.

An automatic watering system is of course the ultimate luxury but will need to be checked to make sure all drippers and sprinklers are functioning properly. The next best thing will be a good friend or neighbour who has been guided through the routine and for whom you can perhaps return the favour. If your carer expresses little interest, prepare and protect whatever you can and keep your fingers crossed. There are techniques to make your plants independent. Give all containers a good soaking and mulch the surface well. Move any delicate plants like ferns and very thirsty plants to a more protected or shadier position, even inside in the sink or bath in similar light conditions, standing on a well-soaked

towel in about 3cm of water. Small pots that contain more hardy plants can be well watered, placed in perforated clear plastic bags, sealed at the top and moved out of the sun. Sticks or skewers will hold the plastic clear of the foliage. This is also excellent for seedlings. An improvised drip watering system can be set up with a large container of water above the plants and wetted strips of cotton or tape draped from this to the soil in individual pots below. If the site is windy, secure both ends of the tapes with stones. Another system is to invert into the soil, a water-filled plastic drink bottle with a small hole in its lid, and let it drain slowly. During holiday breaks pots can stand in saucers of water, but remember to remove them as soon as possible on your return. Do not make your preparations obvious to burglars; obscure as much as you can.

There will be many changes in plant and leaf shape observable when you return. Shrivelled plants can usually be revived by immersing the whole pot in a deep bucket of water, allowing time for the pot, potting mix and root ball to fully engorge once more. Some plants that look finished will recover after this treatment. Prune them back and wait at least two weeks for new leaves to emerge if they are particular treasures, but throw away dismal failures as soon as possible; they ruin the effect. Return plants to their original positions and turn any that have grown sideways to the light. A small tip pruning will set them going straight again. Check for insect damage or disease that may have developed in your absence and control it before it runs amok in the collection.

Under your care and watchful pampering the scene will soon return to normal.

index

Editor *Susan Tomnay*
Designer *Caryl Wiggins*
Illustrator *Richard C.T. Gregory*
Photographer *Leigh Clapp*, except where specified
Publishing manager (sales) *Jennifer McDonald*
Publishing manager (rights and new projects) *Jane Hazell*
Assistant brand manager *Donna Gianniotis*
Pre-press *Harry Palmer*
Production manager *Carol Currie*
Business manager *Sally Lees*

Chief executive officer *John Alexander*
Group publisher *Jill Baker*
Publisher *Sue Wannan*

Produced by *ACP Books*, Sydney.

Printing by Dai Nippon Printing Korea.

Published by ACP Publishing Pty Limited,
54 Park St, Sydney;
GPO Box 4088, Sydney, NSW 1028.
Ph: (02) 9282 8618 Fax: (02) 9267 9438.
acpbook@acp.com.au
www.acpbooks.com.au

AUSTRALIA: Distributed by Network Services,
GPO Box 4088, Sydney, NSW 1028.
Ph: (02) 9282 8777 Fax: (02) 9264 3278.

UNITED KINGDOM: Distributed by Australian Consolidated Press (UK),
Moulton Park Business Centre, Red House Rd, Moulton Park, Northampton,
NN3 6AQ Ph: (01604) 497 531 Fax: (01604) 497 533 acpukltd@aol.com

CANADA: Distributed by Whitecap Books Ltd,
351 Lynn Ave, North Vancouver, BC, V7J 2C4, Ph: (604) 980 9852.

NEW ZEALAND: Distributed by Netlink Distribution Company,
Level 4, 23 Hargreaves St, College Hill, Auckland 1, Ph: (9) 302 7616.

Balconies, Courtyards and Pots
Includes index.
ISBN 1 86396 139 9.
1. Gardening.
(Series: Australian Women's Weekly gardening series).
635

© ACP Publishing Pty Limited 1999
ACN 053 273 546
This publication is copyright. No part of it may be reproduced or transmitted
in any form without the written permission of the publishers.
First published 1999. Reprinted 2002.

Cover: *A pot of pink calla lilies is set in a wooden bowl and
behind in a wire basket are agapanthus. Both pots are concealed
with Spanish moss mulch.*
(Photo © Libelle)

Back cover clockwise from top left: *canna lily, page 28;
group planting, page 26; ball of colour, page 75;
courtyard collection, page 98.*
(Photos *Leigh Clapp*)

Acknowledgments

Our thanks go to Rob Willis and his team at Belrose Nursery, NSW Australia, for
their generous assistance in providing us with pots and plants, helping with plant
identification, and allowing us to photograph in the nursery. Also thanks to
Arizona Cacti Nursery for help with some cacti identification, and to all the other
nurseries and gardeners for generously allowing us to photograph their gardens.

World climate zones

Use this map to locate areas of the world with a climate similar to your own.
Plants from those regions are most likely to be successful in your garden.

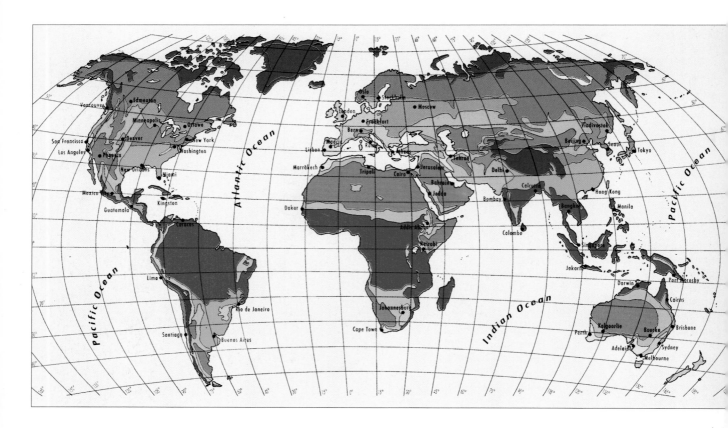

TUNDRA Average summer temperature 0 – 10°C (32 – 50°F). Very severe winters.

SUB-ARCTIC Severe winters. Average temperature above 10°C (50°F) for less than four months.

COLD CONTINENTAL Rain year-round or dry winters. Average summer temperatures below 22°C (72°F).

COOL CONTINENTAL Severe winters but warm to hot summers. Average summer temperature 27°C (80°F). May be rainy year-round or dry in winter.

TEMPERATE Cool winters, warm summers. Average summer temperature 16°C (60°F). May be rainy year-round or wet in winter.

SUBTROPICAL Cool to mild winters, warm to hot summers. Average summer temperature 27°C (80°F). May be rainy year-round or dry in winter.

MEDITERRANEAN Cool to mild winters, warm to hot summers. Average summer temperature 27°C (80°F). Summers dry.

SEMI-ARID PLAINS Seasonal or evenly spread low rainfall. Average summer temperature 32°C (90°F). Cold or mild winters.

DESERT Very low rainfall. Average summer temperature 38°C (100°F). Winters may be cold or mild.

TROPICAL Year-round warmth. High humidity, high rainfall, heaviest in summer; winters may be dry or less wet. Average summer temperature 27°C (80°F).